Acclaim for ANATOLE BROYARD's

Kafka Was the Rage

"Lively and amusing . . . a wide-eyed, fond look at a band of eager adventurers . . . making their way through the forests of thought and sex." —*New York Magazine*

"Some writing is so rich that commentary is superfluous, even presumptuous. That's the case with Anatole Broyard." —*Los Angeles Times*

"Greenwich Village was Broyard's Walden Pond. And like *Walden*, this book will become a classic." —Arthur Danto

"Its pages are charged with feeling. . . . [Broyard] was able to move past irony into unabashed nostalgia and . . . makes us long for the Village he too quickly left behind." —Pete Hamill, *The New York Observer*

"A funny, loving, reflective, and astringent memoir. . . . This is Anatole at his best." —Alfred Kazin

"[Broyard is] a gifted, often scintillating writer who . . . seldom fails to reward the reader in delightful and surprising ways." —*Boston Globe*

"Haunting . . . unforgettable . . . [*Kafka Was the Rage*] reveals the texture and contours of [Broyard's] mind . . . and what an excellent critic and consciousness he was." —*Newsday*

"So well executed that this little book seems an essential part of what every New Yorker ought to know about this town." —Stanley Crouch, *Daily News*

Books *by*
ANATOLE BROYARD

Intoxicated by My Illness

Kafka Was the Rage:
A Greenwich Village Memoir

ANATOLE BROYARD

Kafka Was the Rage

Anatole Broyard was a book critic, columnist, and editor for *The New York Times* for eighteen years. He is the author of the critically acclaimed *Intoxicated by My Illness* (Clarkson Potter, 1992). He died in 1990 in Cambridge, Massachusetts.

ANATOLE BROYARD

Kafka Was the Rage

A Greenwich Village Memoir

VINTAGE BOOKS

A Division of Random House, Inc. New York

FIRST VINTAGE BOOKS EDITION, JULY 1997

Copyright © 1993 by Alexandra Broyard

All rights reserved under International and Pan-American
Copyright Conventions. Published in the United States by
Vintage Books, a division of Random House, Inc., New York,
and simultaneously in Canada by Random House of Canada
Limited, Toronto. Originally published in hardcover in the
United States by Carol Southern Books, an imprint of
Crown Publishers, Inc., New York, in 1996.

The Library of Congress has cataloged the Carol Southern
Books edition as follows:

Broyard, Anatole.
Kafka Was the Rage: A Greenwich Village memoir / by
Anatole Broyard.—1st ed. 1. Broyard, Anatole—Homes and
haunts—New York (N.Y.) 2. Greenwich Village (New York,
N.Y.)—Social life and customs. 3. Greenwich Village (New
York, N.Y.)—Intellectual life. 4. Greenwich Village (New York,
N.Y.)—Fiction. 5. Authors, American—20th century—
Biography. I. Title.
PS3552.R7915Z463   1993
809—dc20
[B] 93-7830
CIP
ISBN 0-517-59618-0

Vintage ISBN: 0-679-78126-9

Book design by M. Kristen Bearse
Author photograph courtesy of Alexandra Broyard

Random House Web address: http://www.randomhouse.com/

Printed in the United States of America

PREFATORY REMARKS

I think there's a great nostalgia for life in New York City, especially in Greenwich Village in the period just after World War II. We were all so grateful to be there—it was like a reward for having fought the war. There was a sense of coming back to life, a terrific energy and curiosity, even a feeling of destiny arising out of the war that had just ended. The Village, like New York City itself, had an immense, beckoning sweetness. It was like Paris in the twenties—with the difference that it was our city. We weren't strangers there, but familiars. The Village was charming, shabby, intimate, accessible, almost like a street fair. We lived in the bars and on the benches of Washington Square. We shared the adventure of trying to be, starting to be, writers or painters.

American life was changing and we rode those changes. The changes were social, sexual, exciting—all the more so because we were young. It was as if we were sharing a common youth with the country itself. We were made anxious by all the changes, yet we were helping to define them.

The two great changes that interested me the most were the movements toward sexual freedom and toward abstraction in art and literature, even in life itself. These two movements concerned me not as social history, but as immediate issues in my daily life. I was ambivalent about both of them and my struggle with them is part of the energy of the narrative.

An innocent, a provincial from the French Quarter in New Orleans and from Brooklyn, I moved in with Sheri Donatti, who was a more radical version of Anaïs Nin, whose protégée she was. Sheri embodied all the new trends in art, sex, and psychosis. She was to be my sentimental education. I opened a bookstore, went to the New School under the GI Bill. I began to think about becoming a writer. I thought about the relation between men and women as it was in 1947, when they were still locked in what Aldous Huxley called a hostile symbiosis. In the background, like landscape, like weather, was what we read and talked about. In the foreground were our love affairs and friendships and our immersion, like swimmers or divers, in American life and art. This book is always a narrative, a story that is intimate, personal, lived through, a young man excited and perplexed by life in New York City at one of the richest times in its history.

The tragedy—and the comedy—of my story was that I took American life to heart with the kind of strenuous and ardent sincerity that young men usually bring to love affairs. While some of my contemporaries made a great show of political commitment, it seems to me that their politicizing of experience abstracted them from the ordinary, from the texture of things. They saw only a Platonic idea of American life. To use one of their favorite words, they were alienated. I was not. In fact, one of my problems was that I was alienated from alienation, an insider among outsiders. The young intellectuals I knew had virtually read and criticized themselves out of any feeling of nationality.

While there's a good deal of sexual activity in the book, none of it is casual—all of it is paid for in feeling and consciousness. In connection with both love and art, I always felt what Irving Howe called "remorse over civilization." I think that in some ways I am a dissenter from modern life. I share the nostalgia that plays such a large part in today's fashions, for example, and in today's movies.

My story is not only a memoir, a history—it's a valentine to that time and place. It's also a plea, a cry, an appeal for the survival of city life. There's a sociology concealed in the book, just as a body is concealed in its clothes.

Anatole Broyard
Southport, Connecticut
April 1989

PART ONE

Sheri

1

My life, or career, in Greenwich Village began when Sheri Donatti invited me to move in with her. *Invited* is not the right word, but I don't know how else to describe it. I had just come out of the army and I was looking for a place I could afford when I met Sheri at a party. She had two apartments, she said, and if I understood her way of talking, she was suggesting that I might come and look at one of them.

Sheri Donatti had the kind of personality that was just coming into vogue in Greenwich Village in 1946. This was a time when Kafka was the rage, as were the Abstract Expressionists and revisionism in psychoanalysis. Sheri was her own avant-garde. She had erased and redrawn herself, redesigned the way she walked, talked, moved, even the way she thought and felt.

She was a painter and she looked more like a work of art than a pretty woman. She had a high, domelike forehead, the long silky brown hair of women in portraits, wide pale blue eyes with something roiling in their surface. Her nose was aquiline, her mouth thin and disconsolate, her chin small and pointed. It was the kind of bleak or wan beauty Village people liked to call quattrocento.

Her body seemed both meager and voluptuous. Her waist was so small, it cut her in two, like a split personality, or two schools of thought. Though her legs and hips were sturdy and richly curved, her upper body was dramatically thin. When she was naked it appeared that her top half was trying to climb up out of the bottom, like a woman stepping out of a heavy garment. Her gestures and motions were a slow dance, a parody of classical poses. They were very deliberate, performed at half speed, as if she had to remember each time, to remind herself, how human beings behaved.

Yet with all this, all the affectation, there was something striking about her. She was a preview of things to come, an invention that was not quite perfected but that would turn out to be important, a forerunner or harbinger, like the shattering of the object in Cubism or atonality in music. When I came to know her better, I thought of her as a new disease.

Twenty-three Jones Street was a shabby tenement with iron stairs that gave off a dull boom and padlocked toilets on each landing. There was no bell and the downstairs door was not locked, so I walked up to the second floor as Sheri Donatti had told me to do. When she answered the door, I saw that she was bare-legged and that her dark dress clung rather lovingly to her thighs.

There were three small rooms, with the kitchen in the center. She led me into her studio, as she called it, where there were paintings on the wall and an unfinished canvas on an easel. We sat down and started to manufacture or assemble a conversation. Like everything else about her, her style of talking took some getting used to. She gave each syllable an equal stress and cooed or chanted her vowels. Her sentences had no intonation, no rise and fall, so that they came across as disembodied, parceled out, yet oracular too. She reminded me of experimental writing, of "the revolution of the word" in the little magazines of the thirties. She talked like a bird pecking at things on the ground and then arching its neck to swallow them.

She went in for metaphors and reckless generalizations, the kind of thing French writers put in their journals. Everything she said sounded both true and false. At the same time I could feel the force of her intelligence, and some of her images were remarkable.

It occurred to me that our conversation might be an interview, a test of my suitability as a tenant or neighbor, so I began to inflate my remarks. I was wearing army fatigues and she asked me whether I had been in the war. She said, Did you kill anyone?

No, I said. I wish I had. I would feel further along in life.

Just when I was beginning to think she'd forgotten why I had come, she got up and offered to show me the other apartment, which was just across the hall. I had been looking forward to this moment, imagining myself with a place of my own in Greenwich Village—but in my first glimpse of the other apartment, I realized that my thinking had been too simple. Already I could tell that nothing about Sheri Donatti was simple, that behind each gesture there was another one. Behind the door of the other apartment, for example, there was an enormous old-fashioned printing press. It loomed like a great black animal, a bear or a buffalo, in the little kitchen.

It was an immensely heavy and powerful machine and I could tell by her manner, by the way she presented it, that it was hers. There was more to this Sheri Donatti than I had thought. This was another aspect of her. She was the driver of this locomotive. The thing took up most of the kitchen, which was as big as the other two rooms put together. I felt that I had entered its lair, its den—this behemoth lived here. The apartment was occupied. There was no room for me, unless I slept in its arms.

I glanced into the other rooms, which were piled with boxes, clothes, and paintings. The apartment was chock-full, crammed with stuff. I had the impression that I was being given a riddle or puzzle to solve. How did I fit into this already-congested space? Was she offering me the place or not? I saw that I would have to ask her. Even if it made me feel slow-witted, someone who doesn't understand the form or get the joke, I had to ask her: I can have this apartment?

She smiled at the question she had forced on me.

I'll take it, I said.

I don't know exactly why I took it. The obvious answer was that I wanted Sheri Donatti, but I didn't, so far as I knew. She was attractive, God knows, but my tastes were still conventional. What I felt was not desire but a strong, idle curiosity, a sense that she was the next step for me, that she was my future, or my fate. I was being drafted by Sheri Donatti as I had been drafted into the army.

I went back to Brooklyn, packed my clothes and books and kissed my parents good-bye. They didn't know what to say—I was a veteran now. Though I regretted the lie, I told them I'd have them over to my apartment when it was fixed up. I had called a taxi, and as it pulled away, with them waving, with me waving, I had that sense of finality all young men have under such circumstances.

When I arrived at Jones Street, Sheri showed me where to put my things. She gave me part of a closet in her bedroom and I hung myself up there, so to speak. If this was a seduction, it was very abstract. I acted as if I knew what was happening, but I was watching her for clues. I suppose it had occurred to me that it might turn out this way, but there was never a point where I was conscious of making a decision.

I'll never know why she chose me. As I discovered later, she could have taken her pick from any number of men. Perhaps she saw something in me that I hadn't seen myself—or something she could do with me that I would never have thought of.

Nineteen forty-six was a good time—perhaps the best time—in the twentieth century. The war was over, the Depression had ended, and everyone was rediscovering the simple pleasures. A war is like an illness and when it's over you think you've never felt so well. There's a terrific sense of coming back, of repossessing your life.

New York City had never been so attractive. The postwar years were like a great smile in its sullen history. The Village was as close in 1946 as it would ever come to Paris in the twenties. Rents were cheap, restaurants were cheap, and it seemed to me that happiness itself might be cheaply had. The streets and bars were full of writers and painters and the kind of young men and women who liked to be around them. In Washington Square would-be novelists and poets tossed a football near the fountain and girls just out of Ivy League colleges looked at the landscape with art history in their eyes. People on the benches held books in their hands.

Though much of the Village was shabby, I didn't mind. I thought all character was a form of shabbiness, a wearing away of surfaces. I saw this shabbiness as our version of ruins, the relic of a short history. The sadness of the buildings was literature. I was twenty-six, and sadness was a stimulant, even an aphrodisiac.

But while squalor was all right outside, as an urban atmosphere, domestic dirt brought out the bourgeois in me. It was the first flaw in my new paradise. As far as I could see, Sheri never cleaned the apartment, and for me to do it would have seemed like a breach of contract, or a criticism. I tried to ignore it, to be philosophical. Perhaps the place is squalid, I said to myself, but it's not sordid. What is dirt? I asked, just as in college we had asked, What is matter? Could this substance grinding under my feet be regarded as a neutral element, like sand? Was it like camping to live so close to dirt? After all, I argued, isn't art itself a kind of dirt?

The first night I spent on Jones Street, I woke up before dawn because I had to pee. I shook Sheri and asked her where she kept the key for the toilet in the hall.

Pee in the sink, she said.

There are dishes in the sink.

They have to be washed, anyway.

But I found it difficult to pee in the sink, because the idea excited me.

It was the same way with the bathtub in the kitchen. I could never take a dispassionate view of it; it always remained for me a kind of exhibitionism to sit in a bathtub in front of somebody else. I was the only son of a Catholic family from the French Quarter in New Orleans, and no one is so sexually demented as the French bourgeoisie, especially when you add a colonial twist.

Perhaps the hardest test for me was the way Sheri dressed. Under her outer clothes, there was only a padded bra, because she was ashamed of the smallness of her breasts. She wore no underpants and no stockings, even in winter, and I was tormented by this absence of underpants. When we walked down the street, I imagined her most secret part grinning at the world. For all I knew, she might suddenly pull up her skirt and show herself to the people and the buildings. What if the wind blew; what if she slipped and fell?

She did fall once. It was in a stationery store on West Fourth Street and she fell because she bumped into W. H. Auden. In fact, they both fell. Auden lived around the corner on Cornelia Street and I often saw him scurrying along with his arms full of books and papers. He looked like a man running out of a burning building with whatever of his possessions he'd been able to grab. He had a curious scuttling gait, perhaps because he always wore espadrilles.

He came hurrying into the stationery store just as

we were going out. Sheri was in front of me and he ran right into her. As he wrote somewhere, fantasy makes us clumsy. He also said that the art of living in New York City lies in crossing the street against the lights.

Sheri, who floated instead of walking, was easy to knock over, and Auden had all the velocity of his poetry and his nervousness. She fell backward, and as she did, she grabbed Auden around the neck and they went down together, with him on top. I was so concerned about her skirt flying up that I didn't even stop to think about whether she might have been hurt. She was lying on the floor beneath one of the most famous poets of our time, but I couldn't see the poetry or the humor of it.

She clung to Auden, who was sprawled in her arms. He tried desperately to rise, scrabbling with his hands and his espadrilles on the floor. He was babbling incoherently, apologizing and expostulating at the same time, while she smiled at me over his shoulder, like a woman dancing.

Until this time, most of the sex in my life had had an improvised character. It was done on the run, in borrowed, often inconvenient spaces, sandwiched between extraneous events, like the arrival or departure of parents or roommates, or the approach of daylight. Now I could have, could enjoy, sex whenever I chose. It had evolved from an obsessive idea into a surprising fact, an independent thing, like a monument. It was perpetually there when I had nothing else to do.

I had always believed, perhaps sentimentally, that

lovemaking clarified things, that people came to understand each other through it. Yet it didn't work that way with Sheri—in fact, she grew more mysterious to me all the time.

She made love the way she talked—by breaking down the grammar and the rhythms of sex. Young men tend to make love monotonously, but Sheri took my monotony and developed variations on it, as if she were composing a fugue. If I was a piston, she was Paul Klee's Twittering Machine.

She was like one of those modern black jazz singers who works against the melody and ignores the natural line ends. Most people agree on some kind of rhythm in sex, but Sheri refused all my attempts at coordination. She never had orgasms—she said she didn't want them. I did want them, but I had to get used to arriving at them in a new way. Instead of building or mounting to orgasm, I descended to it. It was like a collapsing of structures, like a building falling down. I remember thinking once that it was the opposite of premature ejaculation.

I had conceived of lovemaking as a sort of asking and answering of questions, but with us it only led to further questions, until we seemed to be locked in a philosophical debate. Instead of the proverbial sadness after sex, I felt something like a semantic despair.

Our sexual progress reminded me of a simultaneous translation. But then, every once in a while, we would speak the same language; she would allow us to chime, to strike the same note at the same time, and it was as if I were suddenly acoustical, resounding, loud in the silence.

When we stayed home in the evenings, I would sit

with a book in my lap and watch her paint. But if she glanced around and saw me reading, she would put down her brush and come over and turn all her art on me. She distrusted books. I never saw her read one. I think she believed I might find something in them that would give me an advantage over her, or that I might use against her.

I felt the same way about her painting. She was an abstract painter and I couldn't follow her there. She left me outside, like a dog that you tie to a parking meter when you go into a store. I had never been comfortable with abstract painting. I had no talent for abstraction, didn't see the need for it, or the beauty of it. Like liberal politics, it eliminated so many things I liked.

Yet if I could understand her paintings, I thought, our sex would be better. We would exist in the same picture plane, pose for each other's portraits, mingle our forms and colors, make compositions. We would be like two people walking through a gallery or museum, exclaiming over the same things.

I began to read up on abstract painting. In the library in the Museum of Modern Art, I rummaged through the shelves, studying for my new life. I had come to think that modern art was an initiation into that life, like the hazing before you get into a fraternity. When I was at Brooklyn College, everyone urged me to join the Communist party, but I refused because I thought it was an uninteresting quarrel with the real. Modern art, though, was a quarrel that appealed to me more. Even if I never got to like it, I enjoyed the terms of the argument. I was impressed by the restless dissatisfaction, the aggressiveness, ingenuity, and pretension of all the theories.

I discovered that you could always find your own life reflected in art, even if it was distorted or discolored. There was a sentence, for example, in a book on Surrealism that stuck in my mind: "Beauty is the chance meeting, on an operating table, of a sewing machine and an umbrella."

2

Taking advantage of the GI Bill, which paid my tuition and gave me a monthly allowance, I enrolled at the New School for Social Research on West Twelfth Street. I'd had a couple of semesters at Brooklyn College before going into the army, but I was bored because I didn't know what I wanted to do with what I was learning. I couldn't see any immediate use for it. But now going to school was part of the postwar romance. Studying was almost as good as art. The world was our studio.

Like the Village itself, the New School was at its best in 1946. After a war, civilization feels like a luxury, and people went to the New School the way you go to a party, almost like going abroad. Education was chic and sexy in those days. It was not yet open to the public.

The people in the lobby of the New School were excited, expectant, dressed to the teeth. They struck poses, examined one another with approval. They had a blind date with culture, and anything could happen. Young, attractive, hip, they were the best Americans. For local color, there was a sprinkling of bohemians and young men just out of the service who were still wearing their khakis and fatigues, as young matrons in the suburbs go shopping in their tennis dresses.

Known as the "University in Exile," the New School had taken in a lot of professors—Jewish and non-Jewish—who had fled from Hitler on the same boats as the psychoanalysts. Because they were displaced themselves, or angry with us for failing to understand history, the professors did their best to make us feel like exiles in our own country. While the psychoanalysts listened in their private offices—with all the detachment of those who had really known anxiety—to Americans retailing their dreams, the professors analyzed those same dreams wholesale in the packed classrooms of the New School.

All the courses I took were about *what's wrong*: what's wrong with the government, with the family, with interpersonal relations and intrapersonal relations —what's wrong with our dreams, our loves, our jobs, our perceptions and conceptions, our esthetics, the human condition itself.

They were furious, the professors, at the ugly turn the world had taken and they stalked the halls of the New School as if it were a concentration camp where we were the victims and they were the warders, the storm troopers of humanism. The building resounded with guttural cries: kunstwissenschaft, zeitgeist and weltanschauung, gemeinschaft and gesellschaft, schadenfreude, schwarmerei. Their accents were so impenetrable that some of them seemed to speak in tongues and the students understood hardly a word.

We admired the German professors. We had won the fight against fascism and now, with their help, we would defeat all the dark forces in the culture and the psyche. As a reaction to our victory, sensitive Americans had entered an apologetic phase in our national life and there was nothing the professors could say that was too much. We came out of class with dueling scars.

I took a course in the psychology of American culture, given by Erich Fromm. Though he had just arrived, he knew America better than we did, because it impinged on him. His *Escape from Freedom,* which had recently been published, was one of those paeans of lyrical pessimism that Germans specialize in, like Schopenhauer, Nietzsche, or Spengler. Sitting on a platform behind a desk, like a judge in criminal court, he passed his remorseless judgment on us. We were unwilling, he said, to accept the anguish of freedom. According to him, we feared freedom, saw it as madness, epistemology run amok. In the name of freedom, we accepted everything he said. We accepted it because we liked the sound of it—no one knew then that we would turn out to be right in trying to escape from freedom.

Fromm was short and plump. His jaws were broader than his forehead and he reminded me of a brooding hen. Yet, like everyone else, I sat spellbound through his lectures. I'll never forget the night he described a typical American family going for a pointless drive on a Sunday afternoon, joylessly eating ice cream at a roadhouse on the highway and then driving heavily home. Fromm was one of the first—perhaps the very first—to come out against pointlessness. It was a historic moment, like Einstein discovering relativity or Heidegger coming up against nothingness.

I also studied Gestalt psychology with Rudolf Arnheim, but here I confess I was disappointed. It seemed to me that Germans were sometimes stunned into a kind of stupor by an ordinary insight, which they would then try to elevate into a philosophy or a system. Colliding with a modest fact in the midst of their abstraction, they just couldn't get over it.

The Gestalt psychologists had discovered that the whole is greater than the sum of its parts—something everybody already knew—and Arnheim spent most of the semester demonstrating this. I kept waiting for him to go on, but he just gave us more experiments, more evidence. It all depended on rats. We never talked about people—only rats. In the advanced courses, it was apes.

Max Wertheimer, the father of Gestalt psychology, made a guest appearance in the class. He was a small man, dressed in a frock coat, and he wore his hair *en brosse*. The high point of his lecture was a demonstration of requiredness, a key term in Gestalt thinking. It meant, if I understood him, that each thing implied other things, or a context, something like a counterpoint of structures. He showed us what he meant with a little experiment of his own. First he taught us a complicated African hand clap, and then when he had us clapping away, he himself set up a weird howling accompaniment.

I attended a special lecture in the auditorium, given by Karen Horney, on the psychology of women. Like Fromm, Horney was a Freudian revisionist. In one of her books, she had said that, in a sense, the neurotic was healthier than the so-called normal person, because he "protested." Protesting was like testifying. Since everyone at the New School proudly considered him- or herself neurotic—it wasn't respectable not to be—Horney's message was just what we wanted to hear.

I don't remember much of the lecture, but it had an unforgettable aftermath. A woman with a fur coat draped over her shoulders rose from her seat and asked a question. But what about penis envy? she said. You haven't said anything about penis envy.

There was a shocked silence. It was like the time, when I was a child, that someone threw a stink bomb in a neighborhood movie house. Horney just sat there on the platform without speaking, gazing at the woman like an analyst contemplating a hopeless patient she had taken against her better judgment.

Her face seemed to swell. She raised one hand above her head and then the other, as if she would try to climb up out of the auditorium and the New School. Then, closing her hands into fists, she slammed them down on the desk. What about it? she said. Her voice rose to a shriek, What about it? I don't have a penis. Can you give me one?

Later, when I was back at the apartment, sitting in my usual chair and watching Sheri paint, I thought about Horney, and it seemed to me that there were lots of other, better things she could have said to the woman. She could have said, Why does everyone think it's so terrific to have a penis? I myself, for example, had a penis, but it didn't help me now to imagine what went on in Sheri's mind as she filled in a ragged area of the canvas with muddy green paint. It seemed to me that a penis was a very primitive instrument for dealing with life. Besides, Horney was wrong. Sheri did have a penis—mine belonged to her more than it did to me.

3

hadn't been living with Sheri very long when Dick
Gilman tried to take her away from me. There was
nothing underhanded about Dick. He simply came
over to the apartment one night and explained that I
was not the right person for Sheri, and that he was.

His opening remarks were so elegant, so hermeneu-
tic, that I didn't realize at first that he was talking about
me. Dick hardly ever referred to real persons, and my
initial impression was that he was describing an unsatis-
factory character in a novel.

When I finally understood what he was doing, I was
more surprised than angry, because I thought of Dick
as a friend. This was no way for a friend to behave. Yet
what he said sounded just like the friendly discussions
of books we carried on in Washington Square or in the
San Remo. And it was this blurring of the boundaries
that confused me.

Dick was odd in a lot of ways. In his reading, for

example, he was a serial monogamist. He'd fall in love with a particular author and remain faithful to him alone, reading everything by and about him. He would become that author, talk like him, think like him, dress like him if possible. If he could find out what his current favorite had eaten and drunk, Dick would eat and drink them, too. He took on his politics, his causes, his eccentricities. At one point in his D. H. Lawrence phase—this was after his Yeats and Auden phases—Dick actually went to Mexico and tried to find Lawrence's footprints in the dust.

He was a very fast reader, so these affairs came and went fairly quickly. No author can survive that kind of identification for long. When he came to the apartment, Dick was still in his Lawrence phase, so perhaps he saw himself stealing Frieda from Ernest Weekley. Could it be that he had fallen for Sheri as he had for Lawrence and Yeats and Auden?

All the same, Dick was a formidable rival—a brilliant talker, an attractive man. He might even have been handsome if his face had not been just a bit vainglorious with all the books he'd read. As Harold Norse, a Village poet, said, "Dick was only twenty-one and he had read more books than Hemingway."

He had told me he was coming to see us and I had thought this meant he wanted to be better friends, because he was rather standoffish and had never visited us before. Now that he was here, I offered him a beer and asked him to take a chair, but he refused both, like a policeman who doesn't drink or sit down while on duty.

He began with a prologue, or prologomenon. He had examined his motives, he said, and was satisfied that they were disinterested. For a moment I thought he was going to say that, like art, he was a mirror held up to nature. What he did say was that I was not serious. There was, he said, an incongruity in my relation to Sheri. At that time we were all very much under the influence of the idea of incongruity in art. But while incongruity was good in art, it was, apparently, bad in life.

We were in the kitchen. Out of a kind of tact, Dick hadn't advanced farther into the apartment. I had taken a chair and Sheri leaned on the metal cover of the bathtub while Dick paced back and forth between the sink and the stove. Since they were only three or four steps apart, he kept whirling around. He was like a lecturer in front of a class, or a peripatetic philosopher. No doubt he had read Nietzsche, who said that the best thoughts come while walking.

Using words like *unconscionable*, he sounded as if he was recommending himself to Sheri more as a critic than a lover. He gesticulated a lot, chopping the air with stiffened fingers, like someone helping to park a car. He had a rather high, cracked voice—the voice of the brilliant talker—and I listened to it with a detached fascination as he explained, in effect, that his sensibility was bigger than mine.

How little he knew about us! He actually saw me as trifling with Sheri, taking advantage of her. As he went on, building his sentences, piling up clauses, I began to get angry. The hell with this, I thought. I ought to punch him in the mouth. But I couldn't. He had turned the situation into a seminar, and you can't punch people in a seminar. Besides, he talked so well—it would be like punching literature in the mouth. And he had a disarming way of appealing to me—to me!—to confirm a point. He was asking me to testify against myself.

Yet even though he addressed himself to me, I don't think he saw me as he marched back and forth ticking off my shortcomings. He was too caught up in his arguments. I was too—they were so persuasive that I began to believe them myself. Yes, I thought, it was probably true—I wasn't right for Sheri. She was too much for me. But that was why I wanted her, why I had to keep her. As Dick described the life she might have with him, I resolved that, if she stayed with me, I would do all the things he was enumerating.

At last, in a splendid peroration, Dick wound up with several striking tropes, like the final orchestral cadences of a classical symphony. He was breathing hard and smiling a little, as if at a job well done. It was impossible to be angry. God bless him, he thought of a woman as a kind of book.

In the silence that followed, it seemed to me that someone should have applauded. I looked at Sheri, who hadn't moved all this time. Her face was unreadable. She was a marvelous actress and knew how to hold the moment. Then, very deliberately, she changed her position a little in leaning on the bathtub, so that she was in an infinitesimally more nonchalant attitude. I was the first to catch on, and when I started laughing, Dick slammed out of the apartment. He could still be heard booming down the iron stairs when I lifted Sheri onto the bathtub cover.

When you look back over your life, the thing that amazes you most is your original capacity to believe.

To grow older is to lose this capacity, to stop believing, or to become unable to believe. When Nemecio Zanarte came to the apartment a couple of weeks later and repeated Dick's performance, I was able to believe at first that he too had simply been struck by Sheri, like Dick.

Nemecio was a Chilean painter. He was tall, dark, thin, and very handsome in the stark, suffering, aristocratic way that only pure Spaniards seem to have. His high, narrow nose and his deep eye sockets were as superbly carved as an El Greco portrait of a cardinal or pope. I imagined that even Nemecio's feet were beautiful, like Christ's in a twelfth-century painted wooden crucifixion.

His voice was soft, deep, and cultivated and his manners were a history of civilization. Yet here he was, like a priest of the Inquisition, invading what was now my home, telling me that, as a gentleman, it was my duty to remove myself and give Sheri her freedom. His English was not fluent and he said "give to Sheri her freedom."

I felt like a man being persecuted. While Dick might be explained as a kind of literary mistake—a misreading?—Nemecio could not. For this exquisitely polite man to do what he was doing, my failings must have been truly flagrant. What was it about me, I wondered, that inspired everyone to interfere in my life? Did I really behave so badly? Could it be that people actually saw Sheri as a quattrocento Madonna?

At least Nemecio had the decency to appear uncomfortable. Personally, he said, he was fond of me—it was not a question of that, but of symmetry. There was not the necessary symmetry between Sheri and myself. His long, graceful fingers moved as he spoke, as if he was trying on gloves. Everything he said could have come right out of Lorca, only his imperfect English spoiled the effect. "Why you don't go?" he said. "As a gentleman, you must go." He kept falling back on that "Why you don't go?" As a speaker, he was not in Dick's class.

He rambled and repeated himself; he seemed to be confused by emotion. His English began to slip and bits of Spanish seeped into his speech. I knew some Spanish, and his enunciation was so fine that I could make out most of what he said. On a certain level, in matters of love, honor, and conscience, all languages are similar.

Nemecio was much better in Spanish. He could make a moral drama of the word *consideración. Apesadumbrar,* which means "to afflict, vex, or grieve," was a beautiful word, too, but it was I, not Sheri, who was afflicted. And each time Nemecio used the word *caballero,* I wanted to say, But I am a *caballero sin caballo.*

I had studied Spanish in school and kept it alive in Spanish Harlem, where I used to go to the Park Plaza on 110th and Fifth to hear the music. When the band played a particularly good piece, the whole audience would cry, *¡Fenómeno!* or *¡Arrolla!*—which means "to gyrate or spin." Now, without thinking, I cried *¡Fenómeno! ¡Arrolla, hombre! ¡Así se habla!*

Nemecio looked at me in astonishment. He hadn't realized that I spoke Spanish, and this put an entirely different complexion on the matter. I was a compadre of sorts, a more civilized creature than he had supposed. He felt that it was impossible now to carry on the deception. His eyes turned to Sheri in a mute appeal. He looked like an exquisite dog, an Afghan or saluki.

Even I, blinded as I was by her, could see that she had put him up to it. After Dick, she got the idea of asking Nemecio too to come over and denounce me. She might even have encouraged Dick in the first place.

Nemecio gave up. He drooped like a flower. *Perdóneme*, Anatole, he said. I have been a fool.

It takes a brave man to be a fool, I said. I was so relieved that I grabbed his hand and squeezed it. And then he was gone.

Well, I thought, what now? On the bathtub cover again? No—absolutely not. I wasn't going to be played with like this. I refused to enter into the game. I refused for all of five minutes.

4

Five or six weeks after moving in with Sheri, I opened a bookshop on Cornelia Street. This was something I had decided to do while I was in the army. It started with some money I made on the black market in Tokyo, where a suit of GI long johns brought $120. I was thinking about what I might do with the money.

I was working the night shift in Yokohama harbor and I was lonely, cold, and bored. Yokohama was a sad place that had been flattened by bombs and the inhabitants were living in shacks made of rubble, propped up in fields of rubble. Since they couldn't lock up these shacks, they took all their belongings with them when they went out. They carried their whole lives on their backs, wrapped in an evil-smelling blanket or a sack that made them look like hunchbacks.

My outfit, a stevedore battalion, had arrived right after MacArthur, and my first job as a dock officer was to scrape a solid crust of shit off a dock a quarter of a mile long. I didn't realize at first that it was human shit. As I figured it out later, Japanese stevedores and embarking soldiers had had no time for niceties toward the end and had simply squatted down wherever they stood. The entire dock was covered with a layer that was as hard as clay. The rain and traffic had packed it down.

I had my own company of 220 men to supervise the job and I was given 1,500 Japanese who would actually chop the stuff away. We provided them with axes, shovels, sledgehammers, picks, crowbars—whatever we could find. We had no bulldozers. They chopped and scraped for three days and then the Medical Corps hosed down the dock with chemicals.

It was on this same dock, where you could still smell the chemicals, that I was working the night I got the idea of the bookstore. I had two gangs unloading the forward hatches of a ship and I was leaning on the rail, under the yellowish overhead spots. It was about three o'clock in the morning and I felt a million miles from home, from anywhere. For something to do, I was thinking about books, trying to see if I could quote passages or whole poems the way some people can.

Mostly it was only single lines I remembered, perhaps because I was tired. Wallace Stevens was my favorite poet and I murmured a few scraps from his books to myself: "Too many waltzes have ended." "Apostrophes are forbidden on the funicular." "The windy sky cries out a literate despair." "These days of disinheritance we feast on human heads." It was reassuring to think, in the middle of the night in this foreign place, that there were people in the world who would take the trouble to write things like that. This was another, wonderful kind of craziness, at the opposite end from the craziness of the army.

We were unloading boxes of condensed milk and as I watched a pallet swing over the rail, I thought that when I got home I would open a bookshop in the Village. It would be a secondhand bookshop, specializing in twentieth-century literature. I remember that the idea made me feel warm. I took my hands out of my pockets and squeezed them together. To open a bookshop is one of the persistent romances, like living off the land or sailing around the world.

After a couple of months of looking, I bought out an old Italian junk dealer on Cornelia Street. I paid him three hundred dollars and agreed to move his stock to a new location. I hired a truck and we carried out old boilers, radiators, bathtubs, sinks, pipes of all sizes, and miscellaneous bits and pieces of metal.

Nineteen forty-six was a good time for a second-hand bookshop, because everything was out of print and the paperback revolution had not yet arrived. People had missed books during the war, and there was a sense of reunion, like meeting old friends or lovers. Now there was time for everything, and buying books became a popular postwar thing to do. For young people who had just left home to go live in the Village, books were like dolls or teddy bears or family portraits. They populated a room.

When I left Brooklyn to live in the Village, I felt as if I had acquired a new set of relatives, like a surprising number of uncles I had never met before, men who lived in odd places, sometimes abroad, who had shunned family life and been shunned in turn, who were somewhere between black sheep and prodigal sons of a paradoxical kind. An aura of scandal, or at least of ambiguity, hovered over these uncles, as if they had run away with someone's wife or daughter. There was a flaw in their past, some kind of unhealthiness, even a hint of insanity.

These uncles were, of course, my favorite authors, the writers I most admired. I felt them waiting, almost calling out to me. They were more real than anything I had ever known, real as only imagined things can be, real as dreams that seem so unbearably actual because they are cleansed of all irrelevances. These uncles, these books, moved into the vacuum of my imagination.

They were all the family I had now, all the family I wanted. With them, I could trade in my embarrassingly ordinary history for a choice of fictions. I could lead a hypothetical life, unencumbered by memory, loyalties, or resentments. The first impulse of adolescence is to wish to be an orphan or an amnesiac. Nobody in the Village had a family. We were all sprung from our own brows, spontaneously generated the way flies were once thought to have originated.

I didn't yet see the tragedy of my family: I still thought of them as a farce, my laughable past. In my new incarnation, in books I could be halfway heroic, almost tragic. I could be happy, for the first time, in my tragedy.

I realize that people still read books now and some people actually love them, but in 1946 in the Village our feelings about books—I'm talking about my friends and myself—went beyond love. It was as if we didn't know where we ended and books began. Books were our weather, our environment, our clothing. We didn't simply read books; we became them. We took them into ourselves and made them into our histories. While it would be easy to say that we escaped into books, it might be truer to say that books escaped into us. Books were to us what drugs were to young men in the sixties.

They showed us what was possible. We had been living with whatever was close at hand, whatever was given, and books took us great distances. We had known only domestic emotions and they showed us what happens to emotions when they are homeless. Books gave us balance—the young are so unbalanced that anything can make them fall. Books steadied us; it was as if we carried a heavy bag of them in each hand and they kept us level. They gave us gravity.

If it hadn't been for books, we'd have been completely at the mercy of sex. There was hardly anything else powerful enough to distract or deflect us; we'd have been crawling after sex, writhing over it all the time. Books enabled us to see ourselves as characters—yes, we were characters!—and this gave us a bit of control.

Though we read all kinds of books, there were only a handful of writers who were our uncles, our family. For me, it was Kafka, Wallace Stevens, D. H. Lawrence, and Céline. These were the books I liked, the books that I read, and they wouldn't fill more than a few shelves, so I went over to Fourth Avenue, which was lined with bookshops, and bought books by the titles, the subjects, the bindings, or the publishers. I was given a 20 percent dealer's discount and I thought I could charge my customers fifty cents or one dollar more for the pleasure of finding these books in a clean, well-lighted place. Although I had never read Balzac, I bought a fifty-volume uniform edition of his novels in a red binding with gold-edged pages. I got it for only nineteen dollars.

There were people in the Village who had more books than money, and I appealed to them in the literary quarterlies. Like someone buying a dog, I assured them that I'd give their books a good home. But it was an unhappy business, because many of these people suffered from separation anxiety. Those who were depressed by letting their books go tended to devaluate them, while others who were more in the hysterical mode asked such enormous sums that I knew it was their souls they were selling. Pricing an out-of-print book is one of the most poignant forms of criticism.

Seeing how young I was, everyone gave me advice. Get Christopher Caudwell, they said. Get Kenneth Burke, William Empson, F. R. Leavis, Paul Valéry. Get Nathanael West, Céline, Unamuno, Italo Svevo, Hermann Broch, *The Egyptian Book of the Dead*. Edward Dahlberg, Baron Corvo, Djuna Barnes—get them too. But above all, at any cost, I must get Kafka. Kafka was as popular in the Village at that time as Dickens had been in Victorian London. But his books were very difficult to find—they must have been printed in very small editions—and people would rush in wild-eyed, almost foaming at the mouth, willing to pay anything for Kafka.

Literary criticism was enjoying a vogue. As Randall Jarrell said, some people consulted their favorite critic about the conduct of their lives as they had once consulted their clergymen. The war had left a bitter taste, and literary criticism is the art of bitter tastes.

A thin, intense young man with a mustache came into the shop and instructed me in bibliophilic etiquette. A bookshop, he said, should have an almost ecclesiastical atmosphere. There should be an odor, or redolence, of snuffed candles, dryness, desuetude—even contrition. He gazed at the shelves, the floor, the stamped tin ceiling. It's too clean here, he said, too cheerful.

I had imagined myself like Saint Jerome in his study, bent over his books, with the tamed lion of his conquered restlessness at his feet. My customers would come and go in studious silence, pausing, with averted eyes, to leave the money on my desk. But it didn't turn out like that. What I hadn't realized was that, for many people, a bookshop is a place of last resort, a kind of moral flophouse. Many of my customers were the kind of people who go into a bookshop when all other diversions have failed them. Those who had no friends, no pleasures, no resources came to me. They came to read the handwriting on the wall, the bad news. They studied the shelves like people reading the names on a war memorial.

There was something in the way a particular person would take a book from a shelf, the way it was opened and sniffed, that made me want to snatch it away. Others would seize upon a book that was obviously beyond them. I could tell by their faces, their clothes, by their manners, the way they moved, that they'd misread the book or get nothing out of it. The kind of person who is satirized or attacked in a book is often the very person to buy it and pretend to enjoy it. As Mallarmé said, "If a person of average intelligence and insufficient literary preparation opens one of my books and pretends to enjoy it, there has been a mistake. Things must be returned to their places."

It was the talkers who gave me the most trouble. Like the people who had sold me books, the talkers wanted to sell me their lives, their fictions about themselves, their philosophies. Following the example of the authors on the shelves, infected perhaps by them, they told me of their families, their love affairs, their illusions and disillusionments. I was indignant. I wanted to say, Wait a minute! I've already got stories here! Take a look at those shelves!

While I pretended to listen, I asked myself which were more real—theirs, or the stories on the shelves. "The familiar man makes the hero artificial," Wallace Stevens said. In the commonplaceness of their narratives, some of these talkers anticipated the direction that American fiction would eventually take—away from the heroic, the larger than life, toward the ordinary, the smaller than life.

As they talked on, I thought of all the junk I had carried out of the shop—the boilers, bathtubs, and radiators. These people were bringing it all back—all the clutter, the cast-off odds and ends of their lives. It was more than I had bargained for. Literature was tough enough, with its gaudy sadness, but this miscellany— these heartaches off the street—was too much for me. In the contest between life and literature, life wins every time.

5

Sheri took me to see Anaïs Nin, who lived in the Village at that time. According to her diary, which was published years later, Anaïs had spiritually adopted Sheri, describing her as the ghost of her own younger self. She spoke of Sheri as a disciple. "So they come," she wrote, "out of the stories, out of the novels, magnetized by affinities, by similar characters." Sheri was "an orphaned child of poverty . . . pleading, hurt, vulnerable, breathless." "She talks as I write, as if I had created a language for her feelings."

Anaïs' apartment was a top-floor walk-up on Thirteenth Street. Everyone Sheri knew lived on top floors, probably because it was cheaper, but I thought of them as struggling to get to the light. Besides Anaïs and her husband, Ian Hugo, a pleasant, self-effacing man, there was a young couple whose names I no longer remember. The young man held a guitar across his knees, but you could see that he would never play it, that it was just part of a composition, like the guitars in Cubist paintings.

Though I hadn't yet read anything by Anaïs, I'd heard of her. It was said that she and Henry Miller had once lived on a houseboat on the Seine. Later I would learn that she had attracted Otto Rank, who allegedly trained her as a psychoanalyst, and who asked her to rewrite his almost unreadable books. In New York she had an odd acquaintance with Edmund Wilson. After Mary McCarthy left him, he developed a crush on Anaïs and took her to his apartment, which Mary had stripped of furniture. When he reviewed one of her novels, you could see him struggling between his desire and his taste. As usual, though, she had the last word in her diary. Summarizing their evening together, she said, "He wanted me to help him reconstruct his life, to help him choose a couch. . . . But I wanted to leave."

Anaïs was a medium-sized woman with a very pale face, like a Japanese actress. She was classical-looking, in the sense of a form that has become rigidified. Her hair was dark, straight, parted in the middle and pulled back. Her lipstick was precise, her eyebrows shaved off and penciled in, giving the impression that she had written her own face. Her figure was trim but without elasticity, its movements willed and staccato. She was pretty in the way of women in old black-and-white movies. There was a suggestion of the vamp about her, and, in fact, she was later to become a kind of Theda Bara of modern literature.

It was impossible to guess her age. Her teeth looked false and her face had the arbitrary smoothness of one that had been lifted, but I thought this unlikely. It was possible she lifted it herself by the sheer force of her will.

Yet she was impressive in her way, an evocative figure. She reminded me of the melancholy Paris hotels of expatriate writing and I could imagine her, wearing an ambiguous fur, sitting defiantly, or insouciantly, in a café. While I could not imagine her in bed with Henry Miller, that may have been his fault.

There was an aura about her, a sense that she was holding a séance. The atmosphere was charged with her energy. When she gave me her hand and looked searchingly into my eyes, I could feel her projecting an image of herself, one that was part French, part flamenco, part ineffable. When she said, You are Anatole, I immediately became Anatole in a way I hadn't been before.

As I listened to her talk—for it was understood that she did most of the talking, even if it was to ask us questions—it occurred to me that she and Sheri deformed their speech as Chinese women used to deform their feet. Her talk was pretty much like the things she wrote in her diaries. An entry from this time gives a good idea of what she sounded like: "Think of the ballet exercises. The hand reproduces resistance to water. And what is painting but absolute transparency? It is art which is ecstasy, which is Paradise, and water." Here's another: "It is possible I never learned the names of birds in order to discover the bird of peace, the bird of paradise, the bird of the soul, the bird of desire."

Her conversation flirted with all the arts and settled on none, like someone who doesn't really want to buy a book browsing in a bookshop. I was careful about what I said, because I could see that Anaïs was important to Sheri. I was afraid of coming out with something literal-minded, like, Were you bothered by rats when you lived on the houseboat?

Though Anaïs described Sheri in her diary as a "figure out of the past," I thought that Sheri was a later, not an earlier, version. Anaïs was already out of style, and Sheri was just coming in. Anaïs was like someone at a party, dancing, drinking, and batting her eyes, and Sheri was the morning after the party. Anaïs was unconscious of the picture she made, and Sheri was all consciousness. While Sheri was always listening to herself, always rehearsing and revising, Anaïs had already posed for her statue. She had posed for it without knowing where it would be put up.

Sheri too was watching herself more than she usually did, if that was possible, perhaps because she felt the pull of Anaïs, the temptation to be "magnetized by affinities." With all this doublethinking, with no one simply speaking up, the conversation grew so stilted that Anaïs was forced to bring out a bottle of wine. With a sudden swoop, she deposited the bottle in my hands, together with an old-fashioned corkscrew. The look she gave me made it clear that this was to be a test of sorts—but of what?

I had no choice but to accept the challenge. In what I hoped was a confident, heterosexual manner, I applied myself firmly, but with an ironic awareness, to drawing the cork. When the screw was all the way in, I pulled slowly and steadily on the handle. I did all the usual things, and I did them in slow motion, so it came as a rude shock to me when the handle broke off.

It simply came away in my hand. I was holding the bottle with the screw in one hand and the wooden stump in the other. My first thought was, It's not my fault. I did it right. She can't blame me. Then I tried to fit the handle back on while Anaïs leaned forward and watched me. Was it a trick? I wondered. A Surrealist or

Dadaist joke? She was smiling, as if I had confirmed her intuition about me. I knew that whatever I did, I would confirm her intuition.

I wanted to fling the bottle against the wall, but she was already pressing another corkscrew into my hand, an identical one. I didn't want it, but I didn't see any way of refusing. I gave the thing a little preliminary twist in the air, just to see whether it would hold together. The original screw was still in place and with some trouble I managed to get it out. Then I worked the new one in, even more deliberate now. It took me five minutes to get it all the way in. I turned it evenly, so as not to put any unnecessary stress on the handle.

I pulled very gradually, gently at first, then more strongly. Nothing happened. The cork didn't budge. I couldn't imagine why not—it wasn't as if this was an ancient bottle of wine that had been sealed by time itself. To get a better purchase, I put the bottle on the floor between my feet.

What came next still seems incredible to me. Sometimes I think it didn't actually happen, that my memory is playing tricks. But it did happen: Before my eyes, I saw the corkscrew slowly emerge from the cork. It didn't break off; the cork didn't crumble. The screw simply straightened out, so that I was holding in my hand something that resembled an ice pick.

I felt like a person in a dream. I shook myself, tried to collect my wits, to stop the blush that was rising to my face. What should I have done? What would Henry Miller have done in my place? Otto Rank? Edmund Wilson?

Anaïs took the bottle and the corkscrew and put them on a table. Perhaps she had never meant for it to be opened. She turned and looked at me through narrowed eyes. I can see, she said, that you are a most interesting young man.

In her diary, there was nothing about the corkscrews, but I was described as "handsome, sensual, ironic." I wasn't fooled: All the young men in her diary were handsome, sensual, and ironic.

6

L iving with Sheri was a process of continual adjustment. It was like living in a foreign city: You learn
the language, the currency, the style of the people.
You find out how to make a phone call, how to take
the subway, where the stores and restaurants are, the
parks, the public pissoirs, the post office. You try to
feel like a native, not a foreigner; you progress from
grammar to idioms in an attempt to talk as if you belonged. Still, you never succeed in feeling at home. You
remain a visitor, perhaps only a tourist.

There was always something else, something more,
another even larger adjustment to be made. She would
come out with a new twist that meant I had to start all
over. When she announced one day that she had a bad
heart, it was as if she had been saving this for last.

It was nighttime and we were in bed. She grew very
inventive at night; she ran through in a rush all the day's
unused possibilities, the leftovers of her sensibility. I

was almost asleep when she came out with her revelation: You know, I have a bad heart.

Of course, I didn't take in at first what she was saying. There was no context for it, no natural leading up. Just You know, I have a bad heart, as if she was saying, Good night, or Move over a little. It was dark and statements in the dark are different.

Also, I never knew whether she was speaking literally or figuratively. As I've already mentioned, she liked to talk in metaphors. I've never known anyone who used so many figures of speech. So when she said, I have a bad heart, I thought she meant as opposed to a good heart, a bad heart as in bad faith, a hard or black heart, a disloyal heart.

She liked to make me work at interpreting her. Not knowing exactly what she meant, I would give her credit for things she had never even thought of. It was like when I used to read Surrealist poetry in French— I imagined all sorts of marvels until I began to use a dictionary.

I was half asleep. We had made love and I was feeling empty, or, rather, *filled* with emptiness, replete with it. But I roused myself and tried to think—not about what she said but what was *behind* it, what she was driving at. I've always been rather literal-minded and it's one of the things I'm ashamed of, as some men are ashamed of the size of their penis.

Why do you think it's bad? I said. Do you feel you're getting softhearted?

I must be careful about climbing stairs, she said. The doctor thinks stairs are dangerous.

Doctor? I said. What doctor? What are we talking about?

I'm telling you, she said, that I have a bad heart. It's defective, wanting, imperfect. The doctor advises me to avoid undue exertion.

My first thought was that I represented undue exertion—we had, in fact, just been exerting ourselves—and that we must put an end to it. But then I heard what she had been saying. You mean you're sick? There's something wrong—actually wrong—with you?

That is what I have been trying to tell you.

But why didn't you tell me before? How long have you known this? I got all excited. I wanted her to get a second opinion, to see a heart specialist, but she said she had already done all that. What it came down to, she said, was that her heart was simply different from other people's hearts.

And so I entered upon still another adjustment. I made Sheri my burden. From then on, whenever we went anywhere, whenever we came back to the apartment, I carried her up the stairs. I delivered her, conveyed her. I became her porter as well as her lover. I was even ready to carry her down the stairs, but she said it wasn't necessary.

At first, before I was used to it, she was surprisingly heavy, in spite of her slenderness. You might say that she was metaphysically heavy. I think too that she made herself go limp, a deadweight. She threw her head back, like the women you see being abducted in romantic paintings.

The hardest part was when we went to see people. Many of her friends were painters who lived on top floors in order to get the light. When we arrived, after four or five flights, I would be red-faced and breathless, unable to speak. Because we hadn't told people about her heart, they wondered about me. They thought we had been doing something in the hallway. I began to get a reputation.

After the first shock of her announcement, it seemed almost natural to me that she should have a bad heart. Her rib cage was so narrow. I put my ear to it and listened. While I imagined ordinary hearts to have a beat like bad rock music, Sheri's heartbeat was more like a Chopin étude, a desultory or absentminded strumming.

I had never thought of her as physically strong. Even though her legs and thighs were solid and full, her body seemed to lead a hazardous life, to have a determined fragility. She did not walk—she floated, and none of her movements made any concession to gravity. When I thought about it, it seemed to me that the human heart was a very primitive instrument, a poor piece of plumbing, for such a complicated, arrhythmical creature. It was such a garish, representational thing to have inside her abstract chest—it was as ugly as the velvet bleeding-heart medals I had admired so much when I was a Catholic child in New Orleans.

I enjoyed carrying her. For a few moments she was in my power. And I liked the idea that she was portable. I began to think of love as weight. When I had her in my arms she seemed more tangible, more palpable. If I wanted to, I could throw her down the stairs, or over the rail.

Our lovemaking changed. The need to be gentle introduced an insidious erotic complication. I inserted myself stealthily, like a burglar. I became a sleep-crawler. In one of his lectures at the New School, Gregory Bateson had told us about a South Pacific tribe that practiced what they called sleepcrawling. The sleep-crawler, or *moetotolo*, visited his lover in her own hut in the middle of the night. This was a tribe that slept in straw baskets to keep away mosquitoes, and the *moetotolo* had to squeeze into the girl's basket and perform without making any noise. The whole family slept in one room, and if the *moetotolo* was discovered, he would be severely beaten.

I too became a *moetotolo*, performing under duress. Feeling like a killer, explosive as a rocket, enormous, I recoiled my passions back into my own body. My desire rebounded with such an impact that I feared for my own heart.

7

I t may have been the German professors at the New School who put the idea in my head—I don't know —but, for whatever reason, I decided to be psychoanalyzed. In New York City in 1946, there was an inevitability about psychoanalysis. It was like having to take the subway to get anywhere. Psychoanalysis was in the air, like humidity, or smoke. You could almost smell it. The whole establishment had moved to New York in a counterinvasion, a German Marshall Plan.

The war had been a bad dream that we wanted to analyze now. It was as if we had been unconscious for three or four years. Once the war was over, we began making private treaties with ourselves. We demanded nothing less than unconditional surrender from life, or to it. There was a feeling that we had forgotten how to live, that the requirements would be different now. Also, I still had some of the money from my black-market dealings in Tokyo. It was found money, so I thought I would spend it in the black market of personality.

Most people went into analysis because they were unhappy—or at least they thought they were. Yet as far as I knew, I was not unhappy. In fact, it appeared to me that I had just about everything I wanted. But I was like an immigrant who goes from a poor country to a rich one and can't quite believe in his new prosperity. I distrusted my happiness—it seemed too easy and I was afraid it might be simply a failure of consciousness. My imagination itched and I had nothing to scratch.

Could it be, I asked myself, that I was happy under false pretenses? Or that I was mistaking sheer youthfulness, pure energy, for happiness?

There was something else, too, almost too vague to describe, like a shadow on my happiness. I was aware of something like static in my head, a sense that some part of me was resisting, or proceeding under protest. There was a dissonant hum or crackle, a whispering in my molecules. My nerves—I suppose it was my nerves —gave off a high, faint whirring, like the sound that billions of insects make in the tropics at night. It was a disturbance as remote as grinding your teeth in your sleep. Or it was as if my brain had something stuck in its teeth. It may have been merely the friction of consciousness, but I chose to see it as a symptom.

It reminded me, this whirring, of the sound of an AC-DC converter. A lot of the tenement apartments in the Village had these converters, because the buildings were originally on direct current and they'd never been changed over. Since most appliances ran on alternating current, you had to get a converter, a machine about the size of a hatbox. You could pick up a secondhand one for about thirty-five dollars.

The trouble with them was that they made a noise, not a loud noise but a penetrating one. People put their converters in closets, but you could still hear them whirring or grinding in there. I used to think of the sound they made as the complaint of cheap apartments, like Lorca's "pain of kitchens." The static or whirring in my head was the sound of my converter. But what was I trying to convert? And how could I bring it out of the closet?

One night after class I spoke to Dr. Fromm. I asked him to recommend an analyst, hoping he would take me himself. But he didn't; he sent me instead to Ernest Schachtel, who taught a course in Rorschach interpretation at the New School.

Dr. Schachtel looked like Paul Klee—or at least like a photograph I had seen of him. It pleased me to imagine I was about to be analyzed by Paul Klee. Schachtel was thin, well-dressed, delicate-looking, almost nervous. He impressed me as the sort of man who read Schiller, Heine, and Kleist, who listened to Schubert and Mahler. His expression was melancholy and I supposed he had suffered during the war. What was it like, I wondered, to leave your own country for another, where all you met was the unhappiness and confusion of the people who lived there? Suppose when Americans went to Paris or Florence, the waiters, hotel clerks, and taxi drivers told them their dreams, their fears and nameless angers.

In Dr. Schachtel's apartment on the Upper West Side, there was just a touch of Bauhaus. His furniture was light, almost fragile, and it occurred to me that when Germans weren't heavy, they were often fragile. Like Fromm and Horney, he was revisionist, and that was what I wanted, to be revised. I saw myself as a first draft.

I was not asked to lie on a couch, which disappointed me a little because I had been looking forward to talking like someone lying in bed or in a field of grass. Instead we sat face-to-face, about eight feet apart, an arrangement that had a peculiar affect on me. I couldn't get away from the feeling that it was not I who was being analyzed but my face, which was huge, gaping.

Another thing that made me uncomfortable was the fact that Dr. Schachtel avoided meeting my eyes. His eyes would travel all around the room, as if he heard a fly buzzing and was idly trying to locate it. I thought of his eyes as following a line of dots, like the path they are supposed to take in looking at a painting. When he did turn to me, it was an unfocused, generic sort of look, a skimming glance that slid off the surface of my face.

I supposed he did this for clinical reasons, so as not to distract me, but the lack of contact was just as distracting. It was like playing a game of tag or blindman's buff. Ordinarily, I would have looked away myself, averting my own gaze from what I was saying, but as soon as I saw him avoiding my eyes, I began to chase his.

I don't remember what I talked about in the first hour, because my main concern was not to bore Dr. Schachtel. I was terribly afraid of boring him. I had an unreasonable desire to avoid saying anything he had heard before, which made it almost impossible for me to speak. A successful analysis, I imagined, was one in which you never bored your analyst. In avoiding boredom, you transcended yourself and were cured. I had come there not to free myself of repressions but to develop better ones.

Dr. Schachtel's face was composed in a concentrated neutrality, the outer reflection of what Freud called free-floating attention. Yet it seemed to me that his attention floated too freely, that I didn't sufficiently attract it. Judging by his expression, he was thinking of something else—a poem by Rilke, or a passage by Theodor Lipps on *Einfuhlung*.

It wasn't until our second session—and only at the very end of the hour—that I discovered what I really wanted to talk about. I had been twenty minutes late and Dr. Schachtel appeared to be upset by this. I told him that I had left the bookshop and gone home to change. I used to put on a jacket and tie to see him, because my relation to my personality was still formal at that time. What I didn't tell him was that Sheri had been in the apartment and she had deliberately decoyed me into bed. She knew I would end by talking about her and she wanted to introduce herself in her own way.

I felt shy about telling him the real reason I was late —it was too recent, still warm—so I began talking about the whirring or grinding sound in my head. I used the word *stridulation,* and as Dr. Schachtel was not familiar with it, I treated him to a dissertation on galvanic sounds.

He said nothing, and his eyes roamed the room. He was bored, I thought. He knew all about me without being told—I was as easy to read as a Rorschach blot. I felt I had to do something to redeem myself, but the hour was almost over. I looked at my watch—it was over. I got up and walked to the door. Dr. Schachtel rose, too, which was his way of saying goodbye. I had my hand on the knob, but I couldn't leave. To leave now would have been like leaving my personality scattered all over the floor, like the Sunday *Times*. I hadn't come through, hadn't *worked*. I couldn't bear my own image of myself and I searched for a punch line that would allow me to go in peace.

I looked at Dr. Schachtel standing beside his chair in a fragile, unathletic European way. I'm disappointed in love, I said. And before he could answer or choose not to answer, I was gone.

At my next session, I tried to take it back. I don't know why I said that, I told Dr. Schachtel. I suppose I wanted to make myself important. In fact, my relation to Sheri is just the opposite of disappointing. You might almost say that it's too satisfying.

How are you disappointed? Dr. Schachtel said.

I don't know that I am disappointed, I said. I just blurted that out. Everyone wants to see himself as disappointed—it's the influence of modern art.

Dr. Schachtel resisted the temptation to be drawn into a discussion of modern art, and there was nothing for me to do but to go on. As far as I can see, I said, I have no reason to be disappointed. Yet something doesn't feel right. I don't feel that my happiness is *mine*. It's like I'm happy outside of myself.

What it is you want that you don't have? Dr. Schachtel asked.

I hesitated. I felt like a high jumper poised for his run. And just at that moment, I caught Dr. Schachtel's eyes. They were shuttling across the room, following some secret trajectory of their own, when I caught them and held them as if I had grabbed him by the lapels. It was too good an opportunity to waste. I want to be transfigured, I said.

I don't know whether he was surprised by this, but I was. I had never even used the word *transfiguration* before, as far as I could remember, never thought about it. I didn't know what I meant by it, yet I knew that it was true, that it described how I felt. When I came out with the word, I was like someone who sneezes into a handkerchief and finds it full of blood.

In novels, I said, people are transfigured by love. They're elevated, made different, lifted out of their ordinariness. Think of the men in D. H. Lawrence's novels. Think of Hans Castorp in *The Magic Mountain* —you probably read it in German. They're no longer schoolteachers or engineers or whatever they were before, but heroic figures. They're exalted; they're blessed.

I supposed, I said, that love would change me, too, would *advance* me somehow. Because without that, it's just sex, just mechanics. And while sex is fine—it's wonderful; it can be like flying—it isn't enough. It doesn't explain, doesn't *justify* the whole business. It can't account for two thousand years of poetry, for all the laughing and crying. There has to be something else, something more. Otherwise, love wouldn't be so famous; we wouldn't be carrying on about it all the time. *It wouldn't be worth the trouble.*

I stopped for breath. Dr. Schachtel's eyes had escaped and I couldn't catch them again. I was confused. I felt that I was back on the deck of a ship in Yokohama harbor talking to myself under the yellow lights. It's not so much to ask, I said. I just want love to live up to its publicity.

I saw Dr. Schachtel eleven times. He was intelligent, astute, even charming, but I never gave him a chance. I suppose that like a good analyst he wanted to see my personality grow, while what I needed was for it to be shrunk to a more manageable size. It was much too big for me.

I insisted on presenting my problems, such as they were, in the abstract, and the abstractions of psychoanalysis were no match for mine. How can I distinguish, I asked Dr. Schachtel, between anxiety and desire? Is sex a defense against art? Is disappointment inevitable, like the death instinct?

What I brought to Dr. Schachtel was not a condition or a situation but a poetics. I wanted to discuss my life with him not as a patient talking to an analyst but as if we were two literary critics discussing a novel. Of course, that's what all patients want, but the irony was that with me it might have worked. It might have been the shortest, or the only, way through my defenses, because I had a literature rather than a personality, a set of fictions about myself.

8

One night while we were making love, Sheri screamed. She had never screamed before, and it took me by surprise. It was a loud scream, right in my face, which was close to hers. Her mouth opened very wide and I could see all the way to the back of her throat, to her uvula. I saw the fillings in her teeth, the far end of her tongue, the shiny red inside of her cheeks.

Her eyes were open, looking at me while she screamed. I thought I must have done something wrong. What's the matter? I said. Are you all right? I knew that women sometimes screamed while making love, but she had never screamed before, and besides, it wasn't like her. I thought I might have hurt her and I stopped what I was doing, even though it was nothing special or unusual. I could have hit a sensitive spot, or maybe she wasn't feeling well.

Is something the matter? I asked, but of course

she didn't answer. She didn't *believe* in questions. But what was I supposed to do? Did she want me to keep on, or stop? I didn't want to stop—I was too far in to stop.

I began again, very gently, hardly moving—and she screamed again. It occurred to me that the neighbors could hear her. I would see those screams in their eyes when we met in the hallway or on the street. But why should she start screaming now? When would I come to the end of her originality? Also, there was something odd about her screams, something not quite right. They were not like the screams you hear in movies, cries torn from the throat. I remembered Fay Wray in *King Kong* —she was a lusty screamer.

Most screams are wide-open vowel sounds—*ah, oh,* or *ee*—that come up from the diaphragm. They're raw and unmodulated, which is why they're startling. But Sheri's screams were not like that. She screamed up in her sinuses, like a factory whistle. It was a blue note, a diphthong.

Her voice sounded hoarse, and I thought of the hoarse cry of the peacock, a phrase from a book. I remembered a line from a Surrealist poem: "The hyena's oblong cry." That's the way my mind was tending.

Sheri's face when she screamed was not screwed up around the eyes or distorted. It was only her mouth that screamed. She wasn't like the girl in the Munch painting whose scream occupies her whole face. Sheri looked as if she was gargling. She let the scream out like an alarm clock that goes off when you can't remember why you set it.

Maybe her screams were meant as a riddle or conundrum. Perhaps she was punctuating unspoken senten-ces. Anything was possible.

It also seemed to me that they were a bit stale, her screams. I got the feeling that she was palming off on me some secondhand screams left over from her old life, her inscrutable past. This is what I was thinking as I lay there, half in, half out.

9

For most of the people in Meyer Schapiro's class at the New School, art was the truth about life—and life itself, as they saw it, was more or less a lie. Art, modern art, was a great, intense, but at the same time vague promise or threat, depending on how you looked at it. If civilization could be thought of as having a sexuality, art was its sexuality.

With the dim stained-glass light of the slides and the hushed atmosphere, Schapiro's classes were like church services. Culture in those days was still holy. If he had chosen his own church, it would have been Romanesque—yet there was something fundamentalist in him, too. He made you want to get up and testify, or beat a tambourine.

I went to him as students twenty years later would go to India. I wanted to believe in something, anything, to become a member of a cult. My family had been neither religious nor cultivated and, coming from New

Orleans, we had always been outsiders in New York. At Brooklyn College, everyone had been a Communist but me.

Modern painting was one more exclusion, one more mystery from which I was shut out. I used to feel this way when people talked about politics, but I didn't mind so much because I wasn't interested in politics. And besides, I secretly thought I was right. I thought that being a Communist was a penalty you had to pay for being interested in politics. It was the adolescence of politics, an awkward stage you had to pass through. But when it came to modern art, I was afraid that maybe the others were right, that I would never be hip or sophisticated, would never belong. I'd never know that smug sense of being of my time, being contemporary.

Perhaps this sounds like a fuss over nothing, but when you're young, everything matters, everything is serious. And besides, I was living with a modern painter, I slept with modern painting. The life we led depended on modern art. Without that, all we had was a dirty apartment.

There were all sorts of stories about Schapiro. It was rumored that the first time he went to Paris he never sat in a café or walked beside the Seine, but spent all his time in museums and libraries. It probably wasn't true, but it fitted him, this story. Reading had turned him into a saint or angel of scholarship, but in some ways I suspected that he was a martyr too, a Saint Sebastian shot through with arrows of abstraction. A rival critic said that Schapiro loved not paintings but the explanations they made possible, and that he valued a painting in proportion to the ingenuity you needed to appreciate it.

Schapiro was about forty at the time. He was a slender, medium-sized man with a classically handsome Semitic face, bony and ascetic, but lit up like a saint's or a martyr's. He wore, as far as I can remember, the same suit all the time, a single-breasted gray herringbone, and he had two neckties.

Like many educated New York City Jews of his generation, Schapiro dentalized his consonants—or perhaps he had a slight lisp that he tried to overcome—and this gave his speech a sibilance, as if he was whispering, or hissing, secrets. The impression of secrecy was increased by the fact that he didn't seem to be talking to us, but to the paintings themselves, like a man praising a woman's beauty to her.

Sometimes he was so brilliant that he seemed almost insane to me; he seemed to see more than there actually was—he heard voices. His knowledge was so impressive as to appear occult. Because he chanted his lectures, he was like a medieval cantor or Gregorian monk.

We were so awed by him that when he said something witty, we were afraid to laugh. It was like the German translators taking the puns out of Shakespeare on the assumption that he had not written them, that they had been added by hacks. I wonder now whether Schapiro ever noticed how tense we were, how pious. Did he realize that students were dropping out all the time, to be replaced by other students?

They didn't drop out because he was disappointing —in fact, it might have been better if he had disappointed us now and then. What drove even his admirers away was a certain remorselessness in his brilliance. It made some of us anxious to think that everything meant something; there was no escape. It was like a fate.

Perhaps the things he said have now become commonplaces of art criticism, but at the time they were revelations to me. And of course he talked about painters like van Gogh, Cézanne, and Picasso, who are old masters today. Then, only forty years ago, they were revolutionaries; we still believed in revolutions.

I remember Schapiro telling us that before Cézanne, there had always been a place in landscape painting where the viewer could walk into the picture. There was an entrance; you could go there, like walking into a park. But this was not true of Cézanne's landscapes, which were cut off absolutely, abstracted from their context. You could not walk into them—you could enter them only through art, by leaping.

Schapiro said that when van Gogh loaded his palette with pigment he couldn't afford, he was praying in color. He put his anxiety into pigment, slapped color into its cheeks. Color was salvation. It had to be thick, and tangible.

One night I smuggled Sheri into the class. It was easy because of all the turnover and the flurry of enthusiasm. The room sloped like a theater and we sat up in the back. Schapiro was going to talk about Picasso, and the place was jammed, with people crouching on the steps in the aisle. Picasso was a perfect subject because there was so much to explain.

Schapiro spoke rapidly, rhythmically, hardly pausing for breath. When he said that with *Les Demoiselles d'Avignon* Picasso had fractured the picture plane, I could hear it crack, like a chiropractor cracking the bones at the base of your neck. As he went on, Schapiro's sentences became staccato, cubistic, full of overlapping planes. I was so excited that I took Sheri's hand in mine.

I felt myself gaining confidence. It was such a relief

to me to know that art could be explained. If I couldn't love art for itself, I could love it, like Schapiro, for the explanations. It was better than never to have loved at all.

He was discussing an early still life of Picasso's, an upended table covered with a white cloth, a bowl of flowers, and a bottle of wine, all paradoxically suspended in space. What we were seeing, Schapiro said, was the conversion of the horizontal plane—the plane of our ordinary daily traversal of life—into an intimate vertical surface of random manipulation.

His voice rose to a cry. He honked like a wild goose. There was delirium in the room. The beam of the projector was a searchlight on the world. The students shifted in their seats and moaned. Schapiro danced to the screen and flung up his arm in a Romanesque gesture. As he spoke, the elements of the picture reassembled themselves into an intelligible scheme. A thrill of gladness ran through me and my hand sweated in Sheri's.

And then we were hurrying down the aisle, stepping over murmuring bodies in the half-light of the screen. We were in the hallway on the second floor, running up the stairs.

On the roof of the New School, there was a deep purplish glow, a Picasso color, the swarthy light that settles on great cities at night. The wind lifted Sheri's hair, but it was not cold for October. The world was warmed by art, like fire.

A low skylight rose up out of the roofline. It was dimmed, an empty studio. The near side was perpendicular, and then it sloped away. Sheri leaned over it, so that the upper part of her body, her head, arms, and shoulders, sprawled down the slope and her sex pointed at the sky. I paused to take a breath and allow my heart to beat. It's a perfect world, I thought, if you understand it. I let the wind pass over us while Sheri gleamed in the dark. When I connected myself to her, we were the chance meeting, on an operating table, of a sewing machine and an umbrella. We converted the horizontal plane into an intimate vertical surface of random manipulation.

10

When I moved in with Sheri, I assumed that now my adult sexual life would begin. Until then, my experience had been limited to what I thought of as collegiate episodes and wartime acts. Now I imagined myself plunging into sex, diving into a great density of things to do. I felt like a person who is about to go abroad for the first time.

But what actually happened was that Sheri and I began not at the beginning, as I had hoped, but at the end of sex. We arrived immediately at a point where, if we had gone any further, what we did would have had to be called by some other names—yoga, mime, chiropractic, or isometrics. We were like lovers in a sad futuristic novel where sex is subjected to a revolutionary program.

Sex has traditionally been associated with joy, which is an old-fashioned, almost Dickensian notion—but Sheri understood, as we do today, that sex belongs to depression as much as to joy. She knew that it is a place where all sorts of expectations and illusions come to die. Two people making love, she once said, are like one drowned person resuscitating the other.

Sometimes I thought of sex as a flight from art, a regression to instinct, but there was no escaping art when I was in bed with Sheri. She reminded me of some lines Wallace Stevens wrote about Picasso. How should you walk in that space, Stevens asked, and know nothing of the madness of space, nothing of its jocular procreations? For Sheri, sex was like space, the jocularity of space. It was a foyer to madness, a little picnic of madness. In her more benign moments, when she was feeling almost sentimental, she was Duchamp's *Nude Descending a Staircase*. She *descended* into my arms. Like art, sex with her was a shudder of hypotheses, a debate between being and nonbeing, between affirmation and denial, optimism and pessimism, illusion and reality, coming and going.

Most people would say that lovemaking is a defense against loneliness, but with Sheri it was an investigation of loneliness, a safari into its furthest reaches. She had a trick of suspending me at a high point of solitariness, when I was in the full flow of that self-absorption that comes over you as you enter the last stages of the act. She would stall or stymie my attempts to go ahead and finish—she'd hold me there, freeze me there, as if to say, See how alone you are! And then I would float above her, and above myself, like an escaped balloon.

Sex with Sheri was full of wreckage. It was like a tenement that has been partly demolished by a wrecker's ball, so that you can see the terrible biological colors people painted their rooms, the pitiful little spaces they chose for themselves. You could see their lives crumbling like plaster. While Sheri and I were lovers, we were also enemies. Each of us hated and feared what the other stood for. In my heart I thought of her as weird and in her heart she saw me as ordinary. We disagreed on most things; all we had in common was desire, perhaps not even that.

She said that I was trying to destroy her. *Destroy* was one of her favorite words. She would stretch it out —destroyyy—as if it was onomatopoetic, as if it made a rending sound. When I answered that I was only trying to understand her, she said that to be understood was a false agreement, like orgasm.

She showed me just enough of herself to keep in touch. She was only physically evident—visible, palpable, audible. I could smell and taste her, although she had hardly any animal effusions. When we were in bed, the only part of me she touched was my penis, because it was the most detached.

I chased her, like a man chasing his hat in a high wind, and she kept blowing away. It wasn't love or desire I felt most clearly with her, but anxiety. She blurred my own sense of what was real, so that I had to keep checking, keep tabulating. I was like someone who, after a shock, feels himself all over. Because Sheri never said, I'm hungry, It's cold in here, or What time is it? I was always on the verge of forgetting that there were such things as hunger, cold, and time, that life was a condition.

Being with her was like having a permanent erection: It aches after awhile. I needed to be bored now and then—boredom is a time for imagining—but she wouldn't let me. She said that boredom was a domestic emotion.

It was as if we were in a race—a race toward some final, all-inclusive formulation. From time to time, I would think I was gaining on her, that we were talking about the same things, turning into a couple, presenting a united front to the world—but then she'd put on a burst of speed and leave me behind. It reminded me of a six-day bicycle race, with first one, then the other forging ahead. We went back and forth like this—and then she simply outdistanced me once and for all. She did this in the middle of the night, while I was asleep— it was like her to present herself as a dream.

I woke up, to find that she was not in the bed. We slept entwined, like interlocking initials, and I was so used to her lying on top of me in the narrow bed that when she wasn't there to hold me down, I floated to the surface of sleep. It was unusual for her not to be in the bed—she never woke in the night. She slept deeply, abandoning herself to it. Sleeping was the only thing she did with abandon, the only time she was anonymous.

As I came awake, it seemed that there was something altered in the room. There was a thinness in the air, a note of sibilance or shrillness, a faint medicinal edge, like the smell of dry cleaning on clothes. Though I couldn't identify it, it was not unpleasant; I didn't mind it. I noticed too that the light was on in the kitchen —it spilled halfway to the bed. I thought that Sheri must be in there, and I got up to see what she was doing.

When I stood up, the smell was stronger, but it didn't mean anything to me because novels are full of the smells of tenements. Then, as I reached the kitchen door, I saw Sheri.

She was sitting on a chair, a wooden kitchen chair. She was naked—we slept naked—and her bare feet rested on the dirty linoleum. Her knees were together and her arms hung down on either side of the chair, which she had pulled over to the stove. She leaned a little to one side to rest her head on the top of the stove, where she had folded a towel for a pillow.

All the gas jets were open. I could hear them hissing —or not exactly hissing, but whispering, emanating. My first thought, of course, was to turn them off, but I hesitated. She had taught me not to be so enthusiastic. To turn them off right away would be to miss the point. There had to be a point to what she was doing. The chair, the towel folded on the stove, the gas—they had to mean something.

Of course it was all like a dream—it had the odd, insistent details of a dream—and I needed to assure myself that I was awake. Then I looked at Sheri to see if she was all right, if she was breathing, but it was difficult to say—everything about the scene was difficult. Her eyes were open and her expression was placid—you'd never have supposed that gas was streaming out a few inches from her face. In fact, she looked like the people in medieval paintings who held their heads on one side— impassive and abstracted. While it occurred to me that she might be in danger, I wouldn't have been surprised to learn that she could breathe gas.

Though I could hear it, though it seemed to be streaming into the room, I was less worried about the gas than I was about getting the point. I gathered myself up and tried to concentrate. I took a deep breath, inhaling the gas, holding it in my lungs like smoke. I took in Sheri's naked body, too, the small breasts and heavy legs, the pallor. I felt the entire apartment thrumming in my head—the dishes in the sink, the dirt on the floor, the paintings on the walls. I could see without looking up the stamped tin ceiling and the plain sheet of tin I had nailed over a hole where a rat had come out.

Standing in the doorway, leaning on the cold jamb, I felt a sudden wash or swoosh of sadness, as if our love was a stove and she was letting all our gas run out. She didn't care about the waste; it didn't touch her. The smell was very strong now and I remembered that she loved to talk about death; she was always comparing things to it, saying that this or that was like death.

She had goose pimples on her skin, and when I looked at my own naked flesh, I saw that I had them, too. Look, I said, we both have goose pimples. I wanted her to see that I was calm, that I could speak in a clear voice. Yet I felt lonely to the point of madness.

I was trying to catch her eye, to make her see me. If she saw me, perhaps she would reconsider, she would turn off the gas herself. She would remember that we had an arrangement, she had invited me to come and live with her. I thought that if she saw me, she might grow nostalgic.

But that was a sentimental idea. The gas was making me sentimental—it was time to turn it off. I threw open all the windows, then I picked her up and carried her to the bed. Think how charming you could be, I said, if you chose to speak. But I knew she wouldn't speak. She never spoke when I wanted her to, only when it didn't matter. I composed myself to sleep because I couldn't think of anything else to do; she tired me out. And as I was dozing off I thought that soon I would have to leave her.

11

Whien I left Sheri I had nowhere to go but Brooklyn. Apartments were still hard to find. Everyone was looking for a place in the Village, like people looking for love. But the last thing I wanted was to return to Brooklyn, even for a little while. I had tasted the city, and I would never be the same. To go back home made me feel like a character in one of those novels reviewers describe as shuttling back and forth in time. I've always disliked those novels.

My parents didn't know about Sheri, so I told them I'd had a three-month sublet and now I was looking for a permanent place. They said yes, of course, they understood that I needed an apartment of my own—I was a veteran now. I don't know what the word meant to them, but they used it all the time. They were forever saying, "You're a veteran now," as if that explained everything, as if I had been killed in the war and this veteran had come back in my place. They were still thinking about the war, but I had already forgotten it. I was a veteran of Sheri, and the war was nothing to me now.

When I first came back from the army, I had seen Brooklyn as a quiet place, a safe place. Now, after living with Sheri in the Village, I didn't see it at all, I walked through Brooklyn without looking, without curiosity. I could only remember being a child there.

I had closed the bookshop. For the first time in my life, I felt a distaste for books. I think it was because my experience with Sheri reminded me too much of the books in the shop. Sheri and I were like a story by a young novelist who had been influenced by Kafka. Everyone was influenced by Kafka in those days. People in the Village used the word *Kafkaesque* the way my parents used *veteran*.

But without the shop, I had nothing to do all day. I wandered around the Village, ringing superintendents' bells, asking about apartments. I sat in Washington Square, watched children skating, pigeons begging, the sun going down. Sometimes I rode on top of the Fifth Avenue bus to 110th Street and back. I didn't want to see any of the people I knew in the Village because they reminded me of Sheri and I knew they would ask me about her.

Then, just when I needed something to do, my friend Milton Klonsky asked me to collaborate with him on a piece he had been asked to write for *Partisan Review*. The piece was on modern jazz, a subject neither Milton nor the editors of *Partisan* knew anything about. Since I had always been interested in jazz, Milton suggested that I write the first draft and he would rewrite it. What he meant was that I'd supply the facts and he'd turn them into prose.

It never even occurred to me to resent this arrangement—I was awed by *Partisan Review* and flattered by Milton's offer. I had never written anything but notes to myself. I was always scribbling on little pads I carried around, jotting down ideas, phrases, images. Half of the young men in the Village were writing such notes. They wrote them in cafés, in the park, even on the street. You'd see them stop and pull out their pads or notebooks to jot down something that had just struck them—the color of the sky, the bend of a street, an incongruity. These notes were postcards to literature that we never mailed.

I took Milton's proposal very seriously. I would go upstairs in my parents' house and listen to jazz for hours, playing records over and over. It suited my mood, which was like the lyrics of a blues song. I had always liked old jazz—from Louis Armstrong to Lester Young—but I hadn't made up my mind about Charlie Parker, who was everybody's hero at that time. While he could be brilliant, I found in Parker's style a hint of the garrulousness that would soon come over black culture.

Also, it seemed to me that jazz relied too much on improvisation to be a full-fledged art form. Nobody could be that good on the spur of the moment. And there was too much cuteness in jazz. It stammered and strained. It took its sentimentality for wisdom.

I tried to imagine what Meyer Schapiro would say about jazz. Was it like *Les Demoiselles d'Avignon,* a fracturing of music, like the splitting of the atom? But there was something momentous, something world-shaking, about the *Demoiselles* that jazz didn't have. It seemed to me that jazz was just folk art. It might be terrific folk art, but it was still only local and temporary.

I found a parallel for jazz not in Schapiro's class but in Gregory Bateson's. Bateson loved to tell stories, and he told them very well. He was in New Guinea, he said, living with the Iatmul tribe, sleeping in a thatched hut on tall stilts, when one morning he was awakened at daybreak by a sound of drumming. He got up and looked out and saw a lone man walking beneath the clustered huts of the village, beating a drum. He walked in a curious way, this man, in a sawtooth pattern—not turning around to keep to his pattern but stepping backward, heels first. And in counterpoint to his drumming, he chanted a sad, staccato recitative.

Bateson learned that this man had suffered a grievance that he could not get settled. The tribe had rejected his plea for redress and so he got up every morning and rehearsed his complaint to the village. He tried to wake them, to disturb their rest, invade their dreams. Thinking about jazz, I remembered this man and I thought that jazz musicians were something like that.

I was still going to the New School, which seemed to be proof against my mood of disillusionment. My classes met three nights a week and I attended them with a somewhat more dispassionate air than before. It was on one of these nights, after a session with Meyer Schapiro, that I came home to Brooklyn, to find Sheri sitting on my mother's lap.

I was so struck by this sight that I felt as if I had butted against a glass door, the way people sometimes do when they don't see it. Sheri and my mother made such a grotesque picture that I thought for a moment I was back in Schapiro's class, looking at *Guernica* or a de Kooning.

They were in an armchair in the family room. Sheri was sitting not *with* my mother in the chair, or beside her, but on her. She was perched on her lap, as a bird perches. In spite of her slenderness, Sheri was much bigger than my mother, who looked like a child beneath her. It was like an adult sitting in a child's lap. Because of the way Sheri slanted across her, only my mother's head and shoulders showed; she peered out from behind Sheri. My father was in a love seat across the room.

They were looking at an album of photographs, our family album. I knew those pictures all too well. I could see them in my mind's eye, my sisters and myself posed against chimneys and cornices on black tar rooftops. Sometimes, in one corner of the picture, clothes fluttered on a line, because people still hung clothes on the roof to dry in those days. My father took us up there because he thought he needed more light; he tortured us with light. When the pictures came out, we looked helpless and blind, like deer caught in the high beams of a car.

This was before people learned to take advantage of the camera, to show it only their best side. The light in our family album was like the glare of truth; there were no shadows in it, just as there are none in the photographs on driver's licenses. It paled our faces and darkened our eyes, almost gave us wrinkles. My father—for it was he who always took the pictures—caught us redhanded and barefaced. We looked at the camera as if it was to be our last look, now or never. Because these pictures seemed to me to be absolute, artless, and true, I didn't want Sheri to see them. To see them would be to know too much about me. If she saw me, me as a child, she would molest that child.

I wanted to take the album away from her, but how could I? I couldn't even talk to her under the circumstances. God knows what I would have said, and how she would have replied. All I could do was watch her and try to keep her in some kind of bounds. Sitting next to my father on the love seat, I gazed at her pale, heavy, unstockinged legs with a mixture of apprehension and desire.

My mother was at her worst, almost helpless, in ambiguous situations. She couldn't improvise. She was a planner; she liked to count. I could see that she was nervous with Sheri on her lap; she was gulping for air. Yet I was afraid to interfere. As long as I let her sit on my mother's lap, Sheri would behave up to a point.

My father was, in all things, deliberately different from my mother. He saw himself as a man of great aplomb, equal to any occasion. In the French Quarter, he had been a popular figure, a noted raconteur, a former beau, a crack shot, a dancer, a bit of a boxer. Now he was looking at Sheri with a show of astuteness. He was a builder and he studied her as if she were a blueprint. I had often seen him poring over blueprints, because it was his job to take them from the architect and translate them into practical terms for the carpenters, plasterers, bricklayers, and painters. He would bring the blueprints home and make a great show of rescuing the building from the architect, whom he always represented as a mere boy.

What did he think of Sheri? I wondered. How did he see her? Was she another piece of architectural foolishness, a schoolboy's idea of a woman? He must have found her flimsy; he would have used more lathes, more plaster, more material. He had once told me that he liked Floradora girls, around 180 pounds.

The room was filled with examples of my father's

taste. It was his hobby to make furniture on the weekends in his workshop in the basement. He was always turning out end tables, side tables, and coffee tables. They were beautifully made, indistinguishable from the better furniture in stores, except that there was something heavy or chunky in their design, as if they were meant to be used by Floradora girls. They were too sturdy-looking, too indestructible. You felt they would last forever, that they would bury you.

Giving my father's pieces away was my mother's hobby. As soon as he made a new table, she gave away one of the old ones. The neighborhood was saturated with his tables; by now my mother was giving them to near strangers.

Because of the way Sheri talked, my mother assumed that she was a foreigner. She spoke to Sheri slowly and distinctly, without a trace of her strong New Orleans accent. She even began to sound a bit like Sheri. Anatole loved to play, she said. When he was a little boy, he was always playing. Carried away by the family album, she embarked on a history of my childhood.

I was waiting for my father to speak. I believe that he too took Sheri for a foreigner, and I expected him to come out in French or Spanish. He once told me that he had learned Spanish in Mexico when he was a young man. But he didn't speak to Sheri at all; he was uncharacteristically silent. His eyes were narrowed and his lips pursed, as if he was meditating or shaping a thought, but he never said what it was. Perhaps it was Sheri's position in my mother's lap that put him off. He had changed his attitude and was looking at the two of them in a dreamy sort of way. Unless you kept him busy, he was always dreaming off.

He was not really a conversationalist—what he liked was to tell stories. He fancied himself as an observer, a commentator, a satirist. He was always telling anecdotes. But he couldn't seem to find an anecdote in his repertoire to tell to Sheri. He couldn't *classify* her.

He should never have left New Orleans, but my mother nagged him into it. He had left the French Quarter a popular man, but he got off the train in Pennsylvania Station, to find snow falling and no one there waiting for him. He lived in New York under protest, a protest he never admitted even to himself. He was ashamed to think that he had been pressured into leaving the city he loved.

We had to leave because my grandfather, my father's father, kept seizing our life savings. He was the best-known builder in the French Quarter and he would take a down payment on a job and spend it on horses or women. Then when he had to buy materials, he would seize our life savings. He had persuaded his four sons to give him power of attorney, but my father would have given him the money anyway. And of course he never paid it back.

My father couldn't get accustomed to New York City. Once, for example, he had a man on the job, sent to him by the carpenter's union, who didn't know how to hang a door. My father couldn't understand how a man who didn't know how to hang a door could hire himself out as a carpenter. But when he sent the man home, the union sent him back. Perhaps now, as he looked at her, he was wondering whether I could send Sheri home.

He shifted on the love seat so that he was wedged into one corner. He looked uncomfortable now, strained. He was squinting and his head was pulled back in a peculiar way. It was an odd attitude and yet it was familiar, another image from our album. I could see this image clearly because my mind was abnormally alert. Sheri's presence in the room electrified me and it took me only a minute to go back twenty years and identify that expression on my father's face. It was his "walking on his hands" look.

When we lived in New Orleans, my father would sometimes walk on his hands. A spirit would seize him and he would throw himself down as if he was diving, and then all of a sudden he would be standing on his hands. On a Saturday afternoon when people brought rocking chairs out in front of their houses and everyone was feeling sociable and relaxed, my father would go down on his hands and walk over to one of his friends on the block. Though they would laugh, nobody seemed to think this was strange. Men were more simply physical in those days, athletic in odd ways. Once, on a bet, my father walked all the way around the block on his hands.

The first time I saw my father on his hands, when I was only two or three, I was terrified. It was as if he had turned the whole world upside down. I was afraid he was never going to get back on his feet again, that he had decided he liked it better down there on his hands, like a dog. He had a funny way of looking at us, too, from down there—not inverted, with his eyes at the bottom of his face, as I had expected at first, but peering up, his head thrown back until it seemed to rest on his shoulder blades. It was this looking up that frightened me so, because the veins in his neck stood out as if they'd burst.

Standing on his hands put a lot of strain in his face.

He strained and smiled at the same time, and I thought he was like a monstrous spider scuttling along the ground. Now, wedged into the corner of the couch, he was looking at Sheri this way, as if he was standing on his hands, his neck arched and his head rearing.

Anatole loved to go to school, my mother was saying. According to her, I loved everything. Could it be true? Until I refused to wear it, she sent me to school in a pongee shirt with a ruffled collar. He hated to miss a day of school, she said. One time when he had a cold, I kept him home and he cried and cried.

I cried? Who was this boy? I never heard of him.

He was so skinny, my mother said. I couldn't do anything with him. He wouldn't drink milk unless it had Hershey's chocolate syrup in it. I used to get tonics from the doctor to try to build him up. In the summertime, I bought him books to keep him inside during the hottest part of the day. He was crazy about Tarzan books.

She was going too far. Sheri was beginning to tire of this skinny, loving, namby-pamby boy. She shifted in my mother's lap and her eyes glinted. The chair they were sitting in was an early version of the Barca-Lounger, with a button on the arm for lowering and raising the back. Now, looking straight at me, smiling, she pushed the button and she and my mother fell back into a horizontal position.

Sheri's bare legs flew up, and in that split second while they rose, I thought that now we would see— yes, this was what she had come for. She had come to Brooklyn on the subway, and had searched out our house on a map to show my mother and father that the woman I lived with wore no underpants.

It was only at the last moment that she arrested her

flying legs and held them straight out before her like a gymnast. But her message was unmistakable. It was a warning—she was warning me, and I knew that I would have to do whatever she wanted. I got up and pulled her off my mother's lap and she let the album fall to the floor. I raised the back of the chair and pretended she had pushed the button by accident.

It's late, I said. I'll take Sheri home. My mother got up out of the chair, as if she was afraid Sheri would sit in her lap again, and my father rose too. I felt a terrific desire to explain myself to them, to tell them that it wasn't the way it seemed, I hadn't changed all that much; the pictures in the album were the real me.

I had realized as soon as I saw her in our house that I would have to go with Sheri, but I wished it could have been managed differently. Yet there was no doubt in my mind that I wanted to go. I wanted to spend the night on Jones Street, even though I knew I would have to leave her again.

12

found an apartment at last, on Prince Street between Sullivan and Thompson, which was then the southeastern edge of the Village. It was a tenement like Sheri's, built for immigrants, old and shabby, a tiny top-floor walk-up divided into three little boxes like walk-in closets. It was cramped and dingy, but I didn't care. I would make it my own, turn it into a home, a studio, as we used to say, a magic word. I gave the super fifty dollars, bought a sterilized secondhand bed, and moved in. Now, I said to myself, I can start to live. I was always starting to live, another beginning, a final beginning.

I had looked forward so much to having an apartment of my own, had carried the idea around with me so fondly all through the army, that I was astonished to discover, after my first few days there, that I was lonely. I couldn't understand how this could be. It was one thing to feel lonely in Brooklyn or in the army, but how could I be lonely in my own place in Greenwich Village? I hadn't yet realized that loneliness was not so much a feeling as a fate. It was loneliness that walked the streets of the Village and filled the bars, loneliness that made it seem such a lively place.

Looking back at the late 1940s, it seems to me now that Americans were confronting their loneliness for the first time. Loneliness was like the morning after the war, like a great hangover. The war had broken the rhythm of American life, and when we tried to pick it up again, we couldn't find it—it wasn't there. It was as if a great bomb, an explosion of consciousness, had gone off in American life, shattering everything. Before that we had been too busy just getting along, too conventional to be lonely. The world had been smaller and we had filled it.

I thought of Sheri and wondered whether, with all the trouble she gave me, she wasn't better than loneliness. Yet I had been lonely with her too—I saw that now. She wasn't company in the ordinary sense. I was lonely between bouts of desire, between distractions. There was no peace with her. She was like a recurrent temptation to commit a crime.

Whoever had the apartment before me had painted the walls in wide vertical stripes in three different shades of blue. I lay on my sterilized bed and felt blue too, every shade of blue. It shook my faith. It was my first great disappointment as an adult, my first postwar defeat. I rallied briefly and painted the walls grass green. I tacked burlap on the windows, but I was still lonely. It was a green loneliness now.

· · ·

After a while, I went to Sheri's apartment to get some clothes and books I had left there. I picked a time when she wouldn't be home—I knew that if I saw her we might start all over again.

Going back there was more of a shock than I had expected. I came in the door and couldn't get past the kitchen. The place was so dense with images that there was no room for me to move. I felt that I had left Sheri a long time ago, when I was somebody else, younger, wilder. I stood listening in the center of the kitchen, as if she might be coming up the stairs to catch me red-handed, a thief, stealing memories. I saw and felt, as I never had before, what an adventure it had been, she had been. She had taken me in, flaunted her witchcraft. She had shown me the future. She made my head spin.

The dishes were still in the sink. They must have been the same dishes, piled up for all time, that I had peed on my first night there. They were like a sculpture, or a painting of dishes by Magritte, an enigmatic element of modern decor, for we had never eaten a single meal, even breakfast, in the apartment. There was no food of any kind, not even in cans, in the kitchen cabinets.

The bed called to me from the other room. How small it was for all the distances we had traveled in it. We had been like angels dancing on the head of a pin. Leaning on the doorjamb, I gazed at the bed as you gaze in museums, from behind a tasseled cord, at the curtained four-posters of kings and queens.

When I first saw this bed, narrower even than a cot, I asked Sheri whether it opened up and she said no, it didn't. Though I had noticed what seemed to be a double frame, I assumed it was broken and forgot about it.

Now, just for something to do, I reached down and pulled at the frame. It came out easily enough; I didn't see anything wrong with it. There was a lever on one side. When I pressed down, the other half of the bed came up and locked into place.

So she had lied. The realization opened up and locked into my mind like the bed opening and locking into place. But why? The only answer I could think of was that she liked to make difficulties. For her, difficulties were art, an art form—you created them. A lie was more interesting than the truth. She hated plain, ordinary truth—she saw it as a failing, a surrender, even an accusation. The truth, she once said, is for animals; they can smell it.

Perhaps she had lied for fun. I would never know. I'd never be sure of anything about her, and understanding this now, taking in the consequences of this thought all at once, made me feel tired. It brought back the strenuousness of living with her, the terrific effort, the watchfulness. I felt so tired at the memory of it that I stretched out on the bed. How would it feel? I couldn't remember ever being in it without her. I lay there and thought about her. I had always seen her through my excitement, but I wanted to consider her through my fatigue, to look at her through half-closed eyes. I lay on the bed like a patient in a hospital, recovering.

Yet it was also true that she had tried to help me, to make me more elastic, or fantastic, more modern. She had tried to lighten me, to teach me how to float, to rescue me from my simplicity. She had set me a number of riddles or parables to educate me by example, the way you do with children who can't understand abstractions. Like the stairs, for example, carrying her up the stairs—that was one of her lessons. There was nothing wrong with her heart—suddenly I was sure of this. If I had stopped to think about it, I would have known. It was like the bed—she had to find a way to break the monotony. Young men are so monotonous.

How shrewd it was of her to bring her heart into it when she hardly had a heart, to suggest it might fail or break. I had to smile at the picture of myself climbing the stairs, breathless and red in the face, carrying her in my arms. She had given me something to do, a lover's job, a fool's errand.

Always she had opposed my curiosity, and now that she wasn't there to prevent me, I pried into her; I pawed her secrets. I got up and went into the other room to look at her paintings. The one on the easel, the last thing she had done, was called *Anatole's Ontological Conspiracy*. *Ontological* was one of my favorite words—you could hear it every night in the San Remo Bar, where young writers hung out. In one of the books in my shop John Crowe Ransom said that the critic must regard the poem as a desperate metaphysical or ontological maneuver. It was as if we had just discovered not the word but existence itself. In 1946, for the first time, we existed.

I dedicate this painting to you, Sheri had said. I give it to you—it's yours. She gave it to me as if that would make me like it. Now I asked myself whether I did in fact like it, but I couldn't tell; I didn't know. It was a part of her that I couldn't separate from the rest. It may have been the most tangible thing about her—more tangible, for example, than her sex.

It was an abstract painting, of course, huddled or collapsed planes in olive, cobalt blue, and brown against a dark yellow ground. A heavy black line arched over the upper part of the canvas, like a negative of a rainbow. The composition reminded me of doors stacked against a wall, from a building that had been torn down. When she was painting the picture I had watched her, trying to follow her logic, to see how one thing led to another and what kind of decisions it required. I tried to imagine how she described the painting to herself.

When she finished I asked her, What do you feel you've done? How is this painting necessary to you? But she just laughed. You'll never be a man, she said, until you can live without explanations. Death is the only explanation. To be explained, to be understood, is like dying. But it's such a solitary feeling, I said, never to be understood. I think I'd rather be half-understood, or misunderstood, than not to be understood at all.

Sheri's expression at that moment reminded me of Bill de Kooning's answer when he was asked, What does abstract art mean to you? He said, Frankly, I don't understand the question, and then he started to describe a man he had known twenty-four years ago in Hoboken, a German who had always been hungry in Europe:

In Hoboken, this man found a place where you could buy all kinds of stale bread very cheaply—French bread, Italian bread, German bread, Dutch bread, American bread, and Russian black bread. He bought big bags of it and let it get even harder and then he crumbled it and spread it on the floor in his flat and walked on it as though it were a soft carpet.

De Kooning said he'd lost sight of him but then found out many years later from someone who'd run into the man that he had become some kind of Jugend Bund leader and took boys and girls to Bear Mountain on Sundays. He had become a Communist too. I could never figure him out, de Kooning concluded, but now when I think of him, all I can remember is that he had a very abstract look on his face.

It was time to go. I felt myself getting sentimental, snuggling in the apartment, remembering only the good parts. I decided to take the painting. I would take it whether I liked it or not, whether it could be explained or not. I would hang it over my bed, which was much too wide.

I was finding it difficult to settle down on Prince Street. When I was looking forward to it, I thought of my apartment as filled with promise, sunny with promise, a box that I would open to find gifts, to unpack my life. But now that I had it, the apartment seemed to be simply a place to wait. I sat in it, or lay in it, and waited. I didn't even know what I was waiting for. What I needed, of course, was something to do. Going to the New School at night wasn't enough. Sheri had been a full-time job, but now I was unemployed.

I would have liked to invite someone to my apartment, just for an hour or so, to drink a beer or a cup of coffee. A visitor would have helped me to break in the place, but there was no one I could ask. I didn't know any girls beside Sheri, or at least not well enough to invite them to my apartment. Going to a man's apartment was a serious thing in those days. And it didn't seem natural to ask a male friend—men met in bars.

Before long, though, I did have a visitor. One night there was a knock at the door. It was early and I was listening to jazz on the radio, trying to decide what to do with the evening. I had not yet succeeded in spending a single night at home.

I got up to answer the door. I thought it might be Sheri; she might have found out where I lived. I didn't have a phone yet and she might have decided to come over to see me. After all, she had gone to Brooklyn.

But it was a man at the door, a stranger. He was holding something in his hand, showing me something, and I took him for a building inspector or a meter reader. It was my first apartment and I didn't know what to expect. Then I saw that it was a shield he was holding. He was a policeman. I have a complaint against you, he said, after I had identified myself. You'll have to come down to the station.

I immediately felt guilty, and at the same time I told myself that I was innocent. I hadn't done anything, although it sounded almost shameful to put it that way. The detective stood in the doorway sizing me up, then he snapped his fingers. The painting, he said. Bring the painting.

It takes a while for a betrayal to register. At first you deny it. You say, Don't be silly, or It's not possible. Then there's a dead spot, a silence, a regrouping. After that you go slowly, gradually through the character of the other person. You examine all the evidence against the idea of betrayal and you say, No, it can't be.

Then, like a door swinging on its hinges in a draft, you go back over your history together. You begin to imagine betrayal as a hypothesis—an absurd hypothesis, a bad joke. Skeptically, playfully, you concede that the circumstances could be interpreted that way, but only if it was somebody else who was betrayed, not you. And then, suddenly, you know that it's true.

The detective had a car and we rode in silence to the Charles Street station, where we went up a flight of stairs to a large room with wooden desks and pale gray-green walls. Except for us, the room was empty. There wasn't so much crime in those days.

The detective, whose name was something like Scanlon, took the painting from me and stood it on the desk, leaning it against the wall. A Miss Sheri Donatti, he said, had reported the theft of a valuable painting and had named me as the probable perpetrator.

I stared at him because I didn't want to look at the painting, which embarrassed me in that room. It was like the time I had come home to find Sheri sitting in my mother's lap. She specialized in such juxtapositions. I didn't steal it, I said. She gave it to me.

Scanlon shook his head, like a pitcher shaking off a catcher's sign.

The painting is named after me, I said. It's her idea of a joke to pretend that I stole it.

People are always joking, Scanlon said, but the law has to take them seriously.

What am I supposed to do? I said. I didn't ask for a bill of sale when she gave it to me. Do I look like a thief?

Scanlon was wearing a gray double-breasted suit and a pale blue fedora. Detectives had to wear hats in those days as part of their uniform. Now he unbuttoned his jacket. He took off his hat and put it on the desk beside the painting. No, he said, you look like a lover. He swung his feet up onto the desk. He was a big man with big feet. There's an easy and a hard way to do this, he said. The easy way is for you to leave the painting and let me talk to Miss Donatti.

No, I said. The painting is mine; it belongs to me. She gave it to me and whether it's valuable or not, I'm going to keep it. At that moment it seemed that this was the only thing she had ever given me, that she had taken back everything else. It wasn't a question of how much I wanted the painting—it was just that this seemed to be the first clear-cut issue between us, the only time our positions were defined.

Scanlon shook his head again. I think you're being foolish, he said. Unless you give up the painting, I'll have to charge you. And you can't win. You must see that you can't win. All you'll get is a bad scene and a sore heart. It won't be a nice way to remember Miss Donatti.

He was surprising, that Scanlon. He was like an Irishman in a book, like a failed lawyer or a defrocked priest. I wondered whether he specialized in cases like this, quarrels over paintings or books or beds or chairs, to the point where he saw it all as a comedy. I felt a great temptation to tell him the whole story—Sheri's offer of the apartment, the printing press behind the door, the dishes in the sink.

He didn't try to hurry me. He waited as if he had all the time in the world. He leaned back with his feet on the desk and allowed me to imagine Sheri in the police station, sitting in the same chair I sat in now, her face tight with avant-garde indignation, telling Scanlon in her odd speech that I had stolen the painting.

How could she have done it? It was between us, a lover's quarrel, yet she had called the police. She had invited Scanlon into our bed, which was so narrow already. She had broken the rules, rules that all lovers recognized, without which love would have been impossible, unthinkable. But that was what she enjoyed, breaking the rules. It was the only thing she enjoyed—she couldn't forgive me for being law-abiding.

It isn't worth it, Scanlon said. He leaned back in the chair until he was looking at me between his feet. Walk out of here, he said, and you'll see that the streets are full of pale-faced girls.

I couldn't think. I didn't want to think. I was afraid to think.

Well then, Scanlon said. He swung his feet off the desk and put his hat back on. His expression changed; he became brisk and purposeful. He picked up the painting and held it out at arm's length so that we could look at it together from our different sides of the desk. He invited me to see it for what it was—but what was it? I had been trying to decide that since I met Sheri.

He waited while I sat there like a witness on the stand who can't remember. Then he reached out his other hand so that he was holding the painting on either side, trapping it. Watching me all the while, he rotated it, like someone turning a wheel. Then he leaned it against the wall again, wrong side up. Look, he said. Turn them upside down and you can't tell one from another.

What? I stared at him in astonishment and a wave of disgust washed over me. He wasn't smart after all. He was just a cop, an Irish cop.

No, I said, that's not true. It's not that simple. But there was no point in arguing. I wasn't talking to Meyer Schapiro; this wasn't the New School. Anyway, my quarrel wasn't with Scanlon—he was only an innocent bystander, after all, like me. We were just two men puzzled by love and art.

I saw, at last, all at once, with a sadness that had been patiently waiting for me, that I would have to leave the painting. And that wasn't all; it was more than that—I would have to leave Sheri there too, in that room, sprawled on the desk. It wasn't, as Scanlon had said, a nice way to remember her.

PART TWO

After Sheri

13

There were lots of good talkers in the Village—that was mostly what we did—but Saul Silverman's talk had high seriousness. This was one of our favorite phrases. It was from Matthew Arnold, whom none of us had ever read. It's hard to explain what the expression meant to us—each of us would have given a different definition—but I suppose it meant trying to see the world as all of a piece. High seriousness meant being intimate with largeness, worrying on a grand scale. There was an evangelical element in it—Saul thought of ideas in terms of redemption. Our ideas would save us from our sins. He was a type that was fairly common at the time but that seems to have gone out of style.

Talking was such a passionate act for Saul that he had grown a bushy mustache to conceal his mouth. To see the organ of his talk, the words being formed, the working of his lips and tongue, would have been too much. Sometimes he would put his hand over his mouth and speak through his fingers as well as his mustache. He had some kind of adenoidal impediment, so that he threw his head back when he spoke, like a rooster crowing.

Saul reminded me of a boy named Meyer who was in my class in the fourth grade at P.S. 44 in Brooklyn. Meyer was thin, with dark crinkly hair and high, perpetually shrugged shoulders. His features were so emphatically articulated that even when he wasn't doing anything he looked hysterical. When the teacher called on him Meyer would stand up in the aisle and throw his head back and gasp for air, pulling his voice unwillingly through his throat and sinuses and forcing it out of his nose. Once he got it out, his speech was extremely precise. He bit off his consonants and spat them into the room, and I remember thinking, though not in those terms, that it was the jagged precision of the words he used that made them pass with such difficulty.

There were two or three other boys like Meyer in the school—skinny, with hawklike faces, curved noses, and strangled voices. They were all Jewish and I assumed in my mechanistic eight-year-old way that their trouble in speaking had something to do with the structure of their noses. I thought that speech was a kind of wailing for them, a cry of rage and despair. They were torn between the desire to hurl their words in our faces and a tradition of secretiveness. Their speech got as far as their noses, like a head cold, and stopped there.

Though I was a good student, I knew I could never be as smart as those Jewish boys who were strangled by their smartness. They were bred to it—their minds had the quickness of racehorses. They had another advantage too: While I was essentially cheerful, filled with a distracting sociability, there was a brooding sadness in the most brilliant of the Jewish boys that turned them inward and made them thoughtful. I saw them as Martians, creatures from a more advanced planet. Next to them I would always be a southerner, a barbarian. They were at home in the city in a way that I wasn't. Their racing minds were part of its teeming.

You can't say such things now without being called anti-Semitic—yet even with all my Catholic mythologies I don't think that I was anti-Semitic. In the 1920s in New York City everyone was ethnic—it was the first thing we noticed. It was as natural to us as our names. We accepted our ethnicity as a role and even parodied it. To us it was always Halloween. Most of our jokes were ethnic jokes—we hardly knew any other kind. We found our differences hilarious. It was part of the adventure of the street and of the school yard that everyone else had grown up among mysteries. Because we were always surprising to one another, there was an element of formality in our friendships.

I still felt some of this surprise, this formality, this mystery, when I was with Saul. He too had a face like an exclamation and a curved nose that the mustache tried to soften. He was small and slight and already balding, as if he had talked his hair off, had raised his eyebrows so many times that his hair had been pushed back once and for all.

Saul was one of the last of a line of romantic intellectuals. Not satisfied to change the way people thought, he wanted to change the way they felt, the way they were, their desires. He was a reformer at heart, but it was not people's politics he wanted to influence; it was their sensibilities. He thought such changes could be brought about by making distinctions. He saw every-thing as a making of distinctions. He amassed them the way other people amassed money or possessions. He pursued them as some men pursue women. One day, when all the distinctions had been made, we would know what beauty was, and justice.

While we were close friends, there were many things I didn't know about Saul. The war still hovered over us; there was a sense of pushing off from it. Yet I had no idea what Saul had done during the war, whether he had been in the service or exempt for some reason. Though I didn't care one way or the other, it was odd that I didn't know about those three or four years of his life. He had a job after the war, but I couldn't have said what he did. I walked him home all the time, yet I had never been in his apartment. When I picked him up there, he was always waiting for me downstairs.

Occasionally Saul referred in a convoluted, Jamesian way to a female companion, but I never met her, and I sometimes thought that she was only a theory of femininity, a sketch for a character. It was hard to picture Saul with a woman. He never talked about sex, and I wondered whether he made love or distinctions with this shadowy creature.

When he got sick Saul was working on a review for *The New Leader*. Isaac Rosenfeld, who was the book editor, sometimes gave reviews to friends, or friends of friends, even when they hadn't published anything before. This was not as frivolous as it sounds, because the Village was full of young men like Saul who could be trusted to turn out a decent piece. Just as Negroes knew about jazz, Jews were expected to know how to write reviews.

Isaac had given Saul *The Well Wrought Urn*, by Cleanth Brooks, a collection of essays on wide-ranging subjects like romanticism, irony, and great neglected poets, and Saul was rereading all the original texts to refresh his memory. At the rate he was going it would have taken him a year to write the review, a review of one thousand words.

At first when he got sick Saul thought he had the flu, because it was going around. When the symptoms persisted, he suspected mononucleosis. He was tired all the time and we had to give up our late-afternoon walks, when we would stroll through the Village like a couple of peripatetic philosophers.

He disappeared for a while. There was no answer when I called him at home—I didn't have his number at work—and I couldn't imagine where he was. I thought of his invisible female companion and wondered whether he might, after all, be spending his evenings with her.

Then he phoned me from his mother's apartment in Brooklyn. He felt exhausted, he said, and needed someone to look after him. I offered to go and see him, but he put me off. I found out later that he was having tests in the hospital.

A couple of days after that, he called again and asked me to come to Brooklyn. His illness, he said, was serious.

Serious? I said. How do you mean, serious?

He laughed. Then he said, High serious.

Saul's mother was a widow, a small, neat woman with a bony face like his and anxious eyes. She had a painful smile, as if she had been musing on the fact that she

97

belonged to the first generation of Jewish mothers to be categorically discredited by their sons. In the current issue of *Partisan Review* there was a story about a Jewish mother, another widow, who had thrown herself across the door of her apartment, defying her son to return to his tenement in Manhattan without the bag of food she had prepared for him. In his desperation, driven wild by love and rage, the son had beaten her about the head and shoulders with a rolled copy of *The New York Times*. Everybody in the Village was talking about the story, which was by a writer we had never heard of. What a stroke! they were saying—to beat his mother with the *Times*.

Of course Saul's illness, whose exact nature was still unknown to me, put a great strain on his mother. She had taken a position toward it and developed a defensive strategy. Saul would be all right, she said, if he would only let himself relax. She believed that his illness was caused by tension, or even by attention, because, like those Jewish boys in P.S. 44, Saul always paid attention. He never relaxes, she said to me. He thinks too much; he takes the world on his shoulders. She watched him constantly to see whether he was thinking. She had a plan to keep him from thinking, and it was clear that she regarded me as a threat to that plan.

I had blundered into an old debate and it was a relief when Saul suggested that we go for a walk. We hadn't taken a walk together in what was for us a long time. His mother immediately objected that it would tire him —but then she saw in his face that she tired him more. Still, as we put on our coats there was an appeal in her eyes. She was asking me not to take him on an intellectual bender, not to make him think. "You can go to

Prospect Park," she said, grasping at the straw that there was less incentive to think in a park.

The day was sunny and cold, as if Brooklyn had been preserved in a refrigerator for us. Saul was silent for the first few minutes, digesting his mother's absence, adjusting his breathing. He wore a navy blue knitted cap she had insisted on and a heavy, dark, timeless-looking overcoat, like a chesterfield. I had never seen the coat before—it must have been his father's. It was too big for him and muffled his gestures.

Poor thing, he said, still going back to his mother, it's hard on her. She's an intelligent person, yet all her impulses are maternal and stereotypical. She feels the falseness of her position, but she can't help it. She struggles against the stereotype like a woman in labor, but nothing new comes forth.

At the entrance to the park a vendor was selling kosher frankfurters and knishes. The knishes smelled good, but under the circumstances—under what circumstances?—I didn't think it was the right time to eat a knish. With the sun buttering it up, the park was warmer than the street. Though most of the trees were bare, there were enough evergreens scattered around to keep the landscape from looking stripped or naked. Children raced by on skates and bikes, like leaves blowing. People walked dogs and there were squirrels and pigeons along the path.

She keeps running baths for me, Saul said. She tries to drown my thoughts, like kittens.

I was studying him out of the corner of my eye, trying to gauge how sick he was. I didn't feel that I could ask him—his sickness had become a part of his secretiveness, his Jewishness, which was even more pronounced now that he was back in Brooklyn at his mother's house. He didn't look sick, yet there was something in his voice—a remote hilarity—that hadn't been there before. Also—and this was a detail I would notice—his sentence rhythms were different.

Though I hadn't been in Prospect Park for more than ten years, I knew it well. When I was eight or nine I was a great reader of Tarzan books and Prospect Park was later to become my jungle, my Africa. With the odd literalness of young boys I took the word *prospect* in a different sense, as referring to my own prospects, which were as yet wide open.

I used to bicycle to the park from my side of Brooklyn. It was several miles, but this was nothing on my bike. I chased butterflies with a net and mounted them on cardboard squares. Sometimes I rented a boat with money from my newspaper route and rowed to the end of the lake. What I liked especially about Prospect Park was the fact that, once you were well inside, you couldn't see buildings, as you always did in Central Park.

You know, I said to Saul, I used to play here.

So did I, he said. I probably saw you.

What did you think of me? How did I impress you?

Look at that silly goy, he said. What a goyish bicycle.

I used to catch butterflies. I rowed a boat.

He smiled. Yes, you would. If I had seen you I would have pitied and envied you.

He was looking around at the park as if he was taking notes, summing it up, trying to arrive at a definition of the ideal park. He was comparing this one to other parks he had only read about: the Bois de Boulogne, the English Gardens in Munich, the Boboli in Florence. His peculiarities made him so real that I could have hugged him.

The path rose up to a little hill and I noticed that Saul was breathing hard. He was staring, too, staring at the pavement as if he had to concentrate on walking. This was the first real sign of his sickness and it seemed crazy to go on keeping quiet about it. Saul, I said, what is actually the matter with you? How long will it be until you can come back?

He took me by the arm, as if I was the one who was sick, and drew me off the path to a bench overlooking the lake. The bench was placed with an unerring sense of rightness. All by itself on a little curve of the bank, it was overhung by a tree that seemed to embrace it.

Imagine, Saul said when we had settled ourselves, that you're a character in a well-written and original novel, a person remarkable for your poise, wit, and presence of mind.

Gladly, I said. I can think of several such novels, dozens of them, in fact. But what am I to be poised and witty about?

About not making a fuss, he said. I want you to enter into a conspiracy with me, to join a movement, sign a manifesto, against the making of fusses.

This was alarming, but I kept up the sprightliness. Why should I make a fuss?

He pulled off the knitted cap. It wasn't that cold in the sun. His hair was standing up in a funny way. He said, I'm not coming back.

His words went into my head like a shooting pain and I looked away across the lake. People were strolling along a path on the other side. The lake wasn't very wide here and I could see the calm, parklike expressions on their faces. A little boy came up from behind us and threw a stone into the water. A pigeon pecked at a candy wrapper and the wind rustled a dismembered newspaper in the wire trash basket. The homeliness of the park, its sweetness, was so piercing that I felt I had been wasting my life.

When Saul said he wasn't coming back, I was sure that he had tuberculosis. It was thin, intense people like him who got it. He would have to go to a dry climate, Arizona or New Mexico. I said, It's TB you have, isn't it?

He was squeezing the knitted cap in his hands. He plucked a white cat hair from the nap and let it fall from his fingers. No, he said, I haven't got TB. If it were only that. His lips went on moving silently beneath his mustache and as I watched it flutter, I wondered whether he would cut it off now that he was sick. A phrase came into my head: The quality of mercy is not strained.

Saul looked around as if he was afraid of being overheard. He put his hand up and felt his hair. I have leukemia, he said.

Leukemia? I said. The word was so unexpected. It seemed raucous to me, as if a bird—a tropical bird, a parakeet or a toucan—had cried out from one of the bare trees.

I know, he said, I know. Why should I have leukemia? Where did it come from? How did it find me? He made a fist with his left hand and clapped his right hand over it as if he was corking a bottle.

Slow down, I said, you're going too fast. What makes you think you have leukemia? How can you be so sure? You can't get leukemia just by saying it.

I was talking nonsense, yet I hoped to believe it. Let's go back and start from the beginning, I said. You felt sick and you went to the doctor. He examined you, took blood, a urine specimen, and so on and sent them to the laboratory. Then you went back again and he told you that you have leukemia? This is what actually happened?

If we reconstructed the circumstances, two critics, two close readers like us, we might find that the doctor and the lab technicians had made an unwarranted assumption. Saul loved to point out unwarranted assumptions. Sometimes he read books just for the pleasure of laughing at their logic.

I know what you're thinking, he said. I went through the same progression. You're going to tell me that they misread the evidence—as if it was a poem. You're going to remind me of *Seven Types of Ambiguity*. But there is no ambiguity—I've got leukemia. Believe me—I've got it.

I didn't know whether I believed him or not. We never believe such things until they're over. You need leisure to think about tragedy. Maybe you can face it only in the absence of the person, after the fact. Or you can do it only when you yourself are in despair.

You know what it's like? Saul said, coming out of nowhere like that? It's like getting a threatening letter from someone you don't even know. When the doctor pronounced the word *leukemia,* I nearly slapped him in the face. I screamed Fuck! and Shit! But what good does it do to go on like that? I don't see why I should disease the way I speak.

I realize, he went on—he was talking in a rush—I realize that to make a fuss is a normal reaction, but why should we? We're not ordinary people, you and I—I don't see why we should feel obliged to become ordinary now.

He had worked it all out. Like his mother, he had taken a position, developed a strategy. He pulled a handkerchief from his pocket and blew his nose. He made it into a rhetorical gesture. What I'm asking you to do, he said, is to go on being yourself. I need you to be yourself—don't turn pious on me. For the sake of our old conversations, for the sake of our friendship— for the sake of literature, if you like—don't speak to me in a hushed voice. Don't patronize me.

Saul—I began, and he said, Shh. He pushed my voice back into my body, like somebody stuffing a pillow into a pillowcase. I threw my head up, like those boys in P.S. 44, and tried to gasp out an answer—but he wouldn't let me. He raised his hand, and there was a terrific authority in the gesture—he had acquired so much authority.

We stared, or glared, at each other. Wait a minute, I said. Hold on. Can't I have a little outburst?

He dropped his hand. He put it into his pocket to immobilize it. No, he said. No, you can't.

We lapsed into a tender silence in which I went on silently arguing with him. He had talked himself into believing he had leukemia. He had overresearched the subject, like the review. Of course I was arguing with myself as much as with him.

All right, Saul, I said. I won't quarrel with you, because neither of us knows what we're talking about. But just remember this—no diagnosis is final or exhaustive. Whatever you have, there's a treatment for it. This is not the Middle Ages. The tragic sense of life is all well and good, but your mother's right—you think too much. Thinking is a form of hypochondria.

He laughed. Yes, he said, you and my mother. He gazed out over the lake as if he expected to see her rowing there. My mother thinks that literature is killing me, that Kafka, Lawrence, and Céline have undermined my resistance. She thinks I have brain fever, like Kirillov or Raskolnikov. Whatever happened to brain fever?

It really is absurd, he said—that old chestnut, the absurd. Look at me—he slapped his arms and legs—why, I've hardly used this body. It's the shoddy manufacture of the times—I'm practically new and obsolete already. My mother keeps turning to me, waiting for me to explain this absurdity away. I'm such a good explainer. He frowned; he shook his head at his mother. Her will, he said, is a terrible force.

I opened my mouth without knowing what I was going to say and he put his fingers over my lips. It was an astonishingly intimate thing for him to do, like a kiss. You know, he said, I feel so smart. All at once, I understand everything. For example, I see now that the world is a more beautiful place than I had supposed. Look at this park—I've never noticed it. If I had my life to live over again, I'd read more Wordsworth.

He hooked his arms over the back of the bench and crossed his legs. He was settling down into himself. It was clear that he wanted to do the talking, so I sat back and listened. The facts could wait; I could argue with him later. He seemed comfortable now, in full flood, like his old self. I was already thinking in terms of his old self.

Another thing I've realized, he said, is that it's harder for a Jew to die. Forgive me for falling back on the chosen, but there's a certain truth in the old boast. It's harder for us because we expect more; we need more. How irresponsible, how careless it is to die so soon. It's such an unintelligent thing to do. We become doctors to prevent death, lawyers to outlaw it, writers to rage against it. But if you're not Jewish, it's different. It may not be quite so bad, so costly. You can die gracefully, athletically, with a thin-lipped smile and a straight nose. A blond death, a swan dive, a cool immersion. You can die without an accent, without dentalizing.

He paused, listening to the echo of this little speech. He seemed pleased with himself. Words, words, words, he said, that's the only medicine. With an abrupt gesture, he pulled on the knitted cap. My thinking cap, he said. I've got to get back and work on the review. Deadlines!

We got up and walked out of the park. We hadn't gone very far. He slapped me on the back. You're a starcher, he said, skinny but strong. You can fight them off, the Kafkas. Hit them in the kishkas. And remember to read the nature poets—a pastoral a day keeps the doctor away. Don't be so proud of your anxiety.

I was going to walk him home, but he insisted on taking me to the subway. We stood at the top of the stairs and our eyes met for the last time. His were filled with an immense kindness. I apologize, he said, for bossing you around. You see how it is. I can't tell this particular story—I can only edit it.

Saul, I said, I'm confused. I can't think.

Me neither, he said. As Tolstoy remarked when he was dying, I don't understand what I'm supposed to do.

Listen, I said, I'll come back tomorrow. We'll try to sort it out.

He didn't answer. He was looking down the subway steps, which he would never descend again. We stood there without moving while life hummed around us, while traffic rushed by and the sun glinted off the store windows.

No, he said at last. I'd rather you didn't come back. You were terrific today, and so was I—but tomorrow we'd be terrible.

Terrible? I said. I don't know—maybe. Would it be so terrible to be terrible?

He thought about this. He turned it over in his mind, the levels of terribleness. You have no idea how busy I am, he said. They tell me there isn't much time, and I want to finish the review. I'd like to be published.

I knew that wasn't the real reason. He wouldn't let me come back because he couldn't bear the simplicity of being sick, the ordinariness of it. He didn't know how to be ordinary; he had been taught that he was special. To be ordinary might lead to sentimentality, and he was more afraid of sentimentality than he was of being alone. *Sentimental* was the cruelest word in literary criticism. It was a goyish trait, like getting drunk. At that moment, Saul reminded me of a man who is asked on his deathbed to embrace a religion and refuses. There was to be no relenting. For the first time, I saw, with a kind of horror, that books had been everything to him.

He had invited me to stand outside the event with him, as a fellow critic—but I couldn't do it. I wasn't that intellectual. His situation brought out all the homeliness in me, the sloppiness. My feelings had no style. To Saul, my sympathy would have seemed almost bestial, the disorderly impulse of a more primitive civilization. He had always been lofty and distant—why should he change now? It was typical of him to give a new meaning to the expression *critically ill*. If I thought he was escaping into literature, I had to remind myself that literature had been our only intimacy.

We shook hands. We did it like Europeans, our hands held high and our wrists bent. When I went down the stairs, my eyes misted up and I had to hold on to the rail.

The station was empty, yet it seemed to be full of thundering trains. I paced along the platform and asked myself whether I had done everything I could. He had rushed me—there hadn't been time to feel, to think. I wanted to run back up the stairs and go after him, but I was afraid of displeasing him. Though I was young and self-centered and thought I would never die, though I secretly felt it was perverse of Saul to get sick, I loved and admired him. Whether he wanted to hear them or not, there were things I wanted to say to him. How could I go away like this without saying them?

I felt cheated—not only of Saul, my friend, my companion, but of something else, something more. I think it was reality itself I felt cheated of, ordinary reality. It was as if he didn't trust me with it. He was disappearing into the difference between us, into his history. He was saying, You can't understand how I feel, what I am. My tragedy is older and darker than your tragedy. You can't come into my ghetto. But even if this had been true—and I don't know that it was—there were other possibilities open to us. He had always behaved as if understanding was everything.

I rehearsed these things all the way home, fussing and muttering, one of those people who talks to himself on the subway. At Canal Street, I got up and stood by the door. I could see my face in the glass. But where's the catharsis? I said. Where's the catharsis?

He went into the hospital a couple of days after that. When I telephoned him, his mother was always beside the bed. Then one day someone else answered and said that Saul was no longer there. When I called his mother, she said, He's dead. That's the word she used. She pronounced both *d*'s.

14

One night in the San Remo Bar Delmore Schwartz invited me to sit in a booth with him. He was with Dwight Macdonald and Clem Greenberg. I was flattered. I knew Delmore because he had accepted for *Partisan Review* a piece I'd written called "Portrait of the Hipster."

They were talking about the primitive: Picasso, D. H. Lawrence, and Hemingway; bullfighting and boxing. I was a bit uneasy, because my piece was about jazz and the attitudes surrounding it, and I didn't want to be typecast as an aficionado of the primitive. I wanted to be a literary man, like them. I felt too primitive myself to be comfortable talking about the primitive.

Yet I couldn't help showing off a little. I had noticed in taking strolls with Delmore that he was surprised and even impressed by what I thought of as ordinary observations. He seemed to see American life only in the abstract, as a Platonic essence. Sometimes he saw it as vaudeville, but always he saw it *through* something else. He imposed a form, intellectual or esthetic, on it, as if he couldn't bear to look at it directly.

Like many other New York writers and intellectuals of his generation, Delmore seemed to me to have read himself right out of American culture. He was a citizen only of literature. His Greenwich Village was part Dostoyevski's Saint Petersburg and part Kafka's Amerika.

I admired his high abstraction, his ability to think in noninclusive generalizations, but I pitied him too. I thought his was as much a lost generation as Hemingway's and Fitzgerald's—in fact, more lost. While the writers of the twenties had lost only their illusions, Delmore, the typical New York intellectual of the forties, seemed to have lost the world itself. It was as if these men had been blinded by reading. Their heads were so filled with books, fictional characters, and symbols that there was no room for the raw data of actuality. They couldn't see the small, only the large. They still thought of ordinary people as the proletariat, or the masses.

I wanted to be an intellectual, too, to see life from a great height, yet I didn't want to give up my sense of connection, my intimacy with things. When I read a book, I always kept one eye on the world, like someone watching the clock.

Anyway, on this particular evening, I started showing off. I did it partly because it was expected of me and partly because I wanted to. I talked about Spanish Harlem. I had been taken there several times by Vincent Livelli, and old friend of mine from Brooklyn College. He was Italian, but he could speak Spanish and he sometimes taught Latin dancing. There was a Latin dance craze in those days. People went to rumba matinees on Saturday afternoons at midtown clubs and Carmen Miranda sambaed her way through New York City in Hollywood musicals.

I told Delmore, Dwight, and Clem that I'd seen a man killed in Spanish Harlem. It was at a dance given by a young man's club called Los Happy Boys. The victim was a stranger who had tried to enter the dance hall without a ticket. When the ticket taker, a club member called Pablito, tried to stop him, the stranger pulled out a switchblade.

The cry went up that he had killed Pablito, and the whole club descended on the stranger. I saw the whole thing—in fact, I saw it from above, like a box seat—as I was going to the men's room. The dance hall was on the second floor and the men's room was down below. I was going down the stairs where Pablito was taking tickets when the stranger came in.

I watched from above as they knocked him down and began to kick and stomp him. It went on for quite a while and I could hear the wet sound as they kicked him. When it was all over, they pulled out handkerchiefs and wiped the blood off their trousers and shoes. By the time the police arrived there was nothing left of the stranger but a suit of clothes and a shapeless mass. The police were philosophical and no charges were pressed.

Then Pablito reappeared. He had a Band-Aid on his forehead, at the hairline. *¡Cómo,* he said, *que le han matado!* Wow, they killed him! When the club members, the Happy Boys, saw Pablito, they all started to laugh. They rushed at him as if they were going to kill him too, but they were kissing him. They raised him up on their shoulders. Everyone had to see him with their own eyes. Pablito himself was amazed and flattered and a little frightened too that his friends had killed the man. After a while, everyone started laughing. They laughed uncontrollably, pointing to Pablito. He laughed too. Then they went upstairs and started dancing again.

The thing about that scene, I told them, was the economy of it. A man who stabs another man over a seventy-five-cent ticket isn't worth even a shudder of compassion, not even a spasm of revulsion. I didn't feel any pity at all for him. I didn't even think of him as a man. Of course, those were days when violence was uncommon, when it could still be seen as dramatic or moral. What I had seen was an act of tribal solidarity, and it was satisfying in its way to see how much the Happy Boys cared—how they laughed and kissed Pablito, how impressed he was by their anger and grief —and then their fastidiousness as they wiped off their trousers and shoes. As an expression of passion, the incident impressed me, for I was a stranger, too, like the man they killed.

It was the sort of thing Hemingway would write about, I said, or Mailer—yet I didn't trust them with such scenes. They'd make it both more and less than it was. Hemingway would harp on the handkerchiefs. Mailer would reach for philosophy.

I told them another story—about the night when the air was filled with flying chairs. A couple of men had gotten into a fight and the whole place divided into two groups. They were all friends and they really didn't want to fight, so they took up positions at each end of the hall and threw chairs. They were light, cane-bottomed chairs that the audience would drum on, like a chorus, when they got carried away by the music.

The chairs arched through the air like birds flying the length of the hall, birds trapped in a room. There must have been forty or fifty of them, a flight of chairs. Some of them met in midair, as if they were mating on the wing. Then after a while it just stopped. No one seemed to be hurt.

As I told these stories I could see that I was making an impression, that these three literary men saw the Happy Boys as something like the Parisian apache dancers, where men threw women around in a violent acrobatic tango. For all their intellectual sophistication, Village writers were suckers. They were awed by action and passion. They saw Western movies as myths. You'd see them coming out of the Loew's Sheridan with their eyes shining.

Was that true, Dwight said, that part about the handkerchiefs? They liked the story. I could have published it in *Partisan Review*. They wanted to see Spanish Harlem. They wanted to visit the primitive, see it in the flesh.

It was a Friday night and I knew that there was a *gran baile* every Friday, so we jumped into a taxi and went straight up Fifth Avenue, which was a two-way street at the time.

Though my father had played New Orleans jazz on our Stromberg-Carlson phonograph, it was Latin American music that I loved most. I don't know why, because much of it was terrible. The arrangements were full of churning horn sections and awkward staccatoes and the singers, who were almost always male, sang through their noses in a high, pinched tenor.

Yet I loved it. As far back as I could remember I had listened to Xavier Cugat on the radio. I was so devoted to him that I was allowed to monopolize the radio when his regular weekly program came on. When I think about it now, I suppose it was the rhythm section, the drums, that appealed to me. I had always felt that life was a rhythmical process. When I was happy, my rhythms, my tuning, were good—everything danced—and when I was unhappy, I didn't have any rhythm at all. It was my secret conviction that Delmore and the other writer-intellectuals had very little sense of rhythm. It wasn't just that Delmore, for example, was clumsy—it went further than that. As Kenneth Burke said, the symbolic act is the *dancing* of an attitude—and I thought there was something about the way New York intellectuals danced their attitudes. There was not much syncopation in their writing. They stayed too close to the bone and they had turned themselves into wallflowers.

I liked it better when writers danced. Even Hemingway, another clumsy man, knew how to dance, and I can imagine even Gertrude Stein and Alice B. Toklas dancing. Writers used to get more out of simply being. Even Edmund Wilson was always dancing. I remember a scene in one of his journals in which he went dancing alone. He couldn't find any of his friends, so he went to a dance hall on Fourteenth Street and danced with a hostess. And while there's something odd about that, it seemed to me to show that it was necessary to him to keep going, to throw an arm around life and move with it.

The music came pouring out of the entrance to the Park Plaza. It had a kind of crippled syncopation, like a dancer who has one leg a bit shorter than the other. This was before mambo came in. They were still doing the Afro-Cuban rumba, a flinging emphatic version of the Cuban rumba, which I found to be a fussy, cramped, voyeuristic sort of dance, where you peered down at your own feet.

Everybody in the Park Plaza—and there must have been two hundred people there—knew how to dance, and this struck me as a remarkable feat in itself. All good popular dancing is a toying with rhythm, an attempt to respond to it and to transcend, to outdo, it, all at the same time. The bad dancer is a victim of the rhythm. He can respond only by being slavishly obedient, by accepting the rhythm as a drill, or an ordeal. In Afro-Cuban dancing, one dragged the beat, like postponing orgasm, withholding assent, resisting, buying time. Nobody danced on the beat—nothing was ever that simple. Here at the Park Plaza, everyone skillfully toyed with the rhythm, and it was exciting to see so many people triumphing over time, at least for the moment. They all seemed competent. It was like a society with no failures.

The Park Plaza was a large, high-ceilinged, rectangular hall with a balcony on one side over a bar and a bandstand at the far end. Tables and chairs lined the walls. We found a place to sit near the bandstand and I went to get a pitcher of beer.

As I watched them, it was Delmore's reaction I noticed most, because he had such a large face. He was looking at the dancers with a terrific intelligence—but his intelligence bounced off them like someone trying to force his way across the dance floor. I could see that he didn't know what to make of the Park Plaza. So this is the real, he seemed to be thinking, this is what Flaubert meant when he said, *Ils sont dans le vrai*. He looked bemused, as if he was trying to imagine another culture, one in which dancing took the place of books.

The band was playing *Sopa de Pichon*, and I explained that pigeon soup was slang for pot. I translated the first stanza of the song: "If on your wedding day / you're lacking a kidney [pun for *cojon*, "ball"] I advise you to take / some pigeon soup." Most of the songs, I explained, contained puns and double meanings—like the pit humor in Shakespeare.

A tall, beautiful girl in front of us was vibrating one buttock while holding the other still. In elaborately crossing his legs, her partner slipped and fell—but he converted it into a flourish. Or perhaps he hadn't fallen at all. In the middle of the next number, the piano played a long riff called a *montuno* and after that the bongo and conga had a long duet. They were especially good, so when the music stopped, a few of the dancers fell to the foor and closed their eyes in ecstasy and cried, ¡No! ¡No!—meaning, Don't stop, or ¡Fenómeno!

Would you like to dance? I said to my guests. I knew one or two girls who came regularly to the Park Plaza and I offered to find partners for our group. Delmore, who never hesitated to play the crazy, impulsive poet, had a blank look on his face. Clem was sliding his eyes around—not like an art critic, but a tourist. Only Dwight, who was a permanent revolutionary, wanted to dance and appeared to be at home in the Park Plaza. I found him a girl named Dinamita, which appealed to his political tastes, and he gyrated away with her. He didn't know what he was doing, but it didn't matter, because he had rhythm, and also an air of conviction, as if there was nothing in human behavior that was alien to him. Tall, thin, white-haired even then, with glasses and a goatee, he was every inch an intellectual—yet he was something more too. He wasn't standing outside of culture looking in. He was in the thick of it. He felt its rhythm.

Delmore and Clem were different. Younger than Dwight, they were part of the first bookish generation of American writers. They were writer-intellectuals in a sense that Faulkner, Hemingway, and Fitzgerald—and the generation before them—were not. Not even Joyce was an intellectual to the degree that they were.

It worried me, this bookishness of theirs. I was afraid I would never be able to keep up with it. I didn't have the patience to spend whole days reading. I was too restless. And I was too much attracted to the world. I read only for what I *needed* to know, or what gave me pleasure; I never read out of any abstract hunger for knowledge. Also, I was suspicious of bookishness.

When Dwight came back, he announced that Dinamita had drums in her belly.

In the end, though, the Park Plaza disappointed me —not that night, but sometime later. I had often admired a girl there—her name, of course, was Carmen. She was the best female dancer in the place. She was Cuban, with chinky eyes and a jutting ass that looked hard as a rock.

She had a cruel, sullen face that never changed expression as she went through an apparently endless series of improvisations. Like any other young American male, I assumed that she knew more about sex or was closer to it than I was. She could dance so well, I thought, because she could direct her sexuality wherever she pleased.

I desired her, the way you have a desire to go on a safari, or to the South Seas. I desired her as you sometimes hunger for a Mexican dinner that will burn your mouth. I thought of her as a test that I would have liked to pass. Also, she was more authentically *other* than any woman I had ever known.

With one exception, the girls I had slept with had been typically American. The exception was a Japanese girl in a geisha house in Tokyo. But though she was even more foreign to me than Carmen, I didn't find her exciting. She was beyond my understanding. I didn't know what moved her. It was as if I was trying to speak Japanese like the naval officers who came to the geisha houses with phrase books.

But I thought I knew something about Carmen. I thought that she too had drums in her belly, that her life was a strong rhythm. I believed I could learn from her, that I could warm my hands over her flames. It was unlikely, though, because I had nothing to offer her. Those cruel slanting eyes of hers passed right over me. I was so pale to her as to be invisible.

And then one night this all changed. I had come to the Park Plaza with a group. I was their guide, the aficionado. I was with a girl named Sandra, a model, a cover girl in fact. We had taken a table and I was going to the bar to get pitchers of beer when Carmen came up to me and said, Dance with me.

I was so surprised that I gave her a stupid answer. I'm not a dancer like you, I said. I can't dance with you. I was referring to the fact that there was a strict hierarchy in the Park Plaza. You asked a girl to dance only if you were as good as she was. No good dancer would ever accept an invitation from anyone who was not recognized. There was no allowance for sentiment.

Of course I felt that this was true of sex too. I could no more sleep with Carmen than I could dance with her. I don't know what I thought she could do, but I imagined that she was more serious about it, more concentrated than I could ever be. I was afraid of being exposed as a sexual imposter, or something like that. At the same time I wanted to give it a try. I wanted to see whether I could get down to the elemental.

So I took her in my arms and started dancing. I had taken about three steps when she said, Let's get out of here. Without a moment's hesitation, I abandoned Sandra and my friends. We went out and got a cab, and I gave the cabbie my address.

I hate that music, Carmen said, leaning back in the cab. She spoke English almost without an accent, except that she bit off her words.

You hate it? I said. What kind of music do you like?

Classical music, she said. André Kostelanetz, Morton Gould. Then she crooned the entire lyrics to Nat King Cole's "Lush Life."

She wasn't what I had thought, but as I walked up the four flights to my apartment behind her, I looked at her ass, which was right in front of my face, and said to myself that this at least was real.

There were no preliminaries, no desperate grappling. She began immediately to pull off her clothes, the way an actress pulls off her costume when the play is over. It turned out that she was wearing a girdle. When she took it off, her ass filled my little bedroom. It was like those life preservers that expand when you pull the cord.

When she was naked, she spoke only Spanish. In fact, she never stopped talking. *¡Ay, que rico eres! ¡Que sabroso! ¡Que fuerte! Y su cuerpo tan blanco,* and so on.

After that she began to give me instructions. Take me from behind! Harder! Slower! Faster! Wait for me! Don't come until I tell you!

I felt like I was taking a dance lesson. The drums were not in her belly—they were in her commands. I was so occupied with her exhortations that I never got into the spirit of the thing. I remained detached and, as a result, the business went on for quite a while.

¡Hombre, she said, *fenómeno!*

After that I couldn't get rid of her. She would call me up and plead with me on the phone. I'll wash you; I'll powder you. I'll light your cigarettes and bring you a glass of whiskey. She had an interminable list of the things she would do, and none of them interested me. What I had wanted was to cross over into her world, and what she wanted was to enter mine.

15

first saw Caitlin Thomas at a party given by Maya Deren in her apartment on Morton Street in Greenwich Village. I saw only the bottom half of her, her legs, thighs, and cotton underpants, because she was holding her dress up over her head as if she was pulling it off, or hiding behind it like a child. She was dancing, a sort of elememtary hootchy-kootch that didn't have much to do with the fast Haitian drum music that filled the room.

Maya was dancing, too, barefoot, with bells on her ankles. She had just come back from Haiti, where she had been studying Haitian dance and mythology. Maya was also an avant-garde filmmaker, an avant-garde everything. Short, stocky, with a dark red, before-its-time Afro, she looked like a Little Orphan Annie who had been kidnapped once again, this time by art.

While Dylan Thomas was the proclaimed guest of honor, Maya was always the real guest of honor at her parties. She had made sure of this with the tapes of Haitian drumming, because none of the poets and literary camp followers she had invited seemed willing to get out on the floor with her.

So it was *mano a mano* between Maya and Caitlin. I had yet to see Caitlin's angry, intellectual milkmaid's face. I hadn't realized who it was beneath the dress until I asked a slender, elegant young man next to me. That, he said, with an irony that was the chief ingredient of the new American poetry, is Caitlin Thomas.

It was like a war of worlds out there on the floor: the childbearing, cottage-keeping, pub-crawling wife of the Welsh bard against a rising star of Greenwich Village. Caitlin relied on the immemorial argument of bump and grind, while Maya, who wore trousers, danced not exactly to the tapes but to the different drummer of the American art establishment. I wondered who would win and where Dylan was. Was he hiding his face, too?

He was in the bedroom that opened off the studio, in a corner where he was surrounded by slender young men. It was as if they had thrown up a picket fence to protect him, not only from Caitlin but from America, from criticism, from mortality. He was no longer the pretty, pouting cherub of the Augustus John painting, but a man swollen by drink, and by sorrow, perhaps, or poetry. He looked like an inflatable toy that had been overinflated.

You forgot Dylan's faults when you read his poems or heard him recite, but he was not at his best at parties. To him, an American party was like being in a bad pub with the wrong people. He appeared to have no small talk—or hardly any kind. The slender young men bounced off him in disappointment.

123

The party had come to a drumming halt. It was a standoff between Maya and Caitlin. Each succeeded in making the other ridiculous. Never lacking in decision, Maya walked over to Caitlin and tried to usher her off the floor. Caitlin resisted, and one of the guests tried to help Maya remove her, but she broke loose and threw a straight overhand right that Sugar Ray Robinson would not have been ashamed of. It caught the officious guest squarely in the eye and he staggered back with his hand to his face. He would have a shiner as a souvenir of the Thomases. As I looked admiringly at Caitlin, I remembered reading or hearing that she and Dylan often fought and she always won.

Now she was genuinely aroused. Hell hath no fury like a famous poet's wife. Maya had brought back a collection of small ceramic Haitian gods, which were arranged on the mantelpiece, and now Caitlin began hurling these against the wall. If she had really tried, Maya could have rallied enough support by now to stop Caitlin, but she couldn't resist the symbolism of the scene. Plunging her fingers into her curls, she cried, like an Ibsen heroine, She's smashing my universe!

This woke Dylan, who had been dozing on his feet in the bedroom. Caitlin was smashing the universe again. He rushed, or rolled, into the studio and seized her by one arm. Then, leaning back, using his weight, he began to swing her in a wide circle—it was a large room—like a game of the Snap the Whip. It was the only safe way to deal with her. He must have worked it out on previous occasions.

There was a wide opening between the studio and the bedroom and, with a suprising dexterity, Dylan swung Caitlin through it and landed her on the bed, where he immediately sat on her. It was a remarkable performance, like a perfect enjambment in a poem. But he was winded by his exertions—this was more tiring even than writing or declaiming poetry—and Maya gave me the job of holding Caitlin down.

It wasn't easy—she was very strong—so I had to more or less lie on top of her as Dylan had. I held my head back because I thought she might bite me. After a minute or two she stopped struggling and her face grew thoughtful. She looked alert, shrewd, very Welsh. Are you queer? she said.

I was still unsophisticated enough to be annoyed by the question. No, I said. I'm not.

She threw her arms around my neck. Then for God's sake, man, she said, love me! Love me!

She was moving too fast for me. I didn't even know whether she was drunk or sober, and I couldn't think of a clever answer. I looked around and Dylan was standing, his back to us, just a few feet away. That would hardly be cricket, I said lamely, betrayed in my confusion into an antiquated English idiom.

Her face grew savage. Bugger the cricket! she said.

As the most expendable—or the only reliable—person at the party, I was deputized to take Caitlin to the Chelsea Hotel. Dylan was too drunk for such an extended effort—he couldn't Snap-the-Whip her all the way up to Twenty-third Street—and besides, Maya was by no means ready to relinquish him. He was going to have to stand in for the Haitian gods.

Someone had a car and I held on to Caitlin in the backseat. She relaxed and made herself comfortable in my arms. When we reached the hotel the other man drove off right away and I took Caitlin up to their room.

She unlocked the door and turned to me. I'll give you a drink, she said. We looked into each other's eyes. Though I couldn't read hers, I thought she could see what was in mine. She was too much for me, and I knew it. I had no idea what she was offering me. A drink? A surreptitious, secondhand kind of fame? A heart-to-heart talk about Dylan?

I made an awkward little bow. Thank you very much, I said. Another time. As I spoke I ducked and the straight right hand whistled over my head. Pushing her gently so I could close the door, I ran down the stairs.

16

I want you to help me buy a suit, Delmore said. He needed me, he said, because he couldn't look at himself in a mirror. You'll have to hold the mirror up to nature for me. Tell me—he drew both hands down his chest—whether the suit suits me, be my beau. We can walk up to Brooks Brothers, he said. I need the exercise. So we met in Washington Square and started up Fifth Avenue like a parade.

Delmore had a peculiar walk, like Dr. Caligari in the movie. He took short, quick steps, as if he had adopted the European walk of his favorite writers, of Dostoyevski perhaps, as opposed to the loping American style. He walked in sputters, in short manic bursts, like his talk. And he was always bumping into me, because he veered when he walked—when he did anything. When he had pushed me almost into the gutter or up against the buildings, I would drop back and come up on the other side of him.

He was telling me a long and intricate story about Milton Klonsky, who was a friend of his and a much closer friend of mine. The story was untrue from beginning to end, yet anyone who knew Klonsky would probably have believed it. I almost did myself. Even as I laughed at the outrageousness of Delmore's invention, I felt myself slipping. In my mind's eye, I could see Klonsky as Delmore presented him, frowning and expostulating in his pleasantly tinny voice. Klonsky had an inhibition about going to the toilet when anyone was in his apartment, so he and Margaret, the girl who lived with him, had tacitly agreed upon a routine. After breakfast, when Klonsky had drunk several cups of coffee, Margaret would announce that she had errands to run and she would go out for about forty-five minutes.

The scheme worked for a while, but then Klonsky rounded on Margaret one day. Why can't you show a little imagination? he said. It's always the same thing with you—a container of milk, a loaf of bread, a bottle of shampoo, stamps. Surely there's more than that to the life of a young woman in a great city like New York. Why, you don't even write letters—what do you need with stamps?

In Delmore's version, the story, punctuated by giggles, went on for fifteen minutes. His mind tossed off details like a dog shaking off drops of water. The toilet was badly situated; it jutted into the living room like a corner fireplace. It had a perforated door, like a rattan chair. A perforated door!

Except for three or four short stories and a handful of poems, I never thought that Delmore's work was as interesting as his talk. When I knew him, he had already written his best things and most of his talent went into talking. Slander was his genius. Yet his slanders were as lyrical as his best poems. He loved slander as you love the poems and stories you can't write.

Klonsky was already a rich character, but Delmore embellished him. Klonsky had all the personal peculiarities of a very good writer and Delmore exaggerated these to the point where Klonsky took on the behaviorial tics of a bad writer. In Delmore's version of him, Klonsky invariably went too far; he overshot the truth and spilled into obsession. He was like a story whose images are too heavy, whose metaphors are too self-conscious, whose language is strained, and whose technique is outmoded.

When Delmore described anyone, they regressed; they lost their saving graces, their scruples and hesitations. He made everyone Dostoyevskian—but in an anachronistic twentieth-century setting. His favorite trick was to take away their irony and leave them exposed. He was like the grammar-school bully who rips open your fly buttons.

I almost wished that Klonsky would do all the things Delmore described, that he would get them off his chest. Delmore's malice was so brilliant, so unerring, it exalted Klonsky; it freed him to be terrible. It was Delmore who helped me to understand what I came to think of as the malice of modern art.

Meanwhile, as we walked, the city passed unnoticed. Like Samuel Johnson, whom he resembled in many ways, Delmore was not interested in prospects, views, or landscape. He had looked at the city when he was young and saw no need to do it again. He had looked at it in much the same way that he had read John Dos Passos or James T. Farrell.

At Brooks Brothers, we went up to the sixth floor, to the less expensive suits. As we waited for the elevator, with Delmore fidgeting beside me, I was reminded of Dostoyevski's Underground Man, who bought new gloves, a new hat, and a fur collar for his coat—all for the purpose of colliding with an officer on the boulevard where he went for a walk each Sunday. When he met the officer in the crowded street, it was always he who had to give way, and now he was determined to throw himself against this haughty creature. But first his clothes must be equal to the occasion.

Delmore seemed nervous and I began to think he was serious about being unable to look at himself in a mirror. He was wearing a threadbare gray flannel suit and proposed to buy another one just like it. When the salesman asked him what size he wore, Delmore said he didn't know. Unlike the Jews of his father's generation, he regarded the subject of clothing as a somehow gentile business.

The salesman held up a suit and Delmore looked blindly at it. What do you think? he said to me, and I realized that this unworldly man saw me as worldly. I remembered another time when he had asked me for an opinion. We were walking that day too and he asked me to walk him home because he wanted to give me his new book, *Vaudeville for a Princess*. When I objected that he couldn't afford to give everyone a copy of his book, he said, Not everyone—I want to give a copy to you. You have less talent for concealing your opinion than most of my friends—I can get the truth out of you.

At his apartment he pondered for a long time over an inscription for the book. He had once proposed, he said, to write *"hypocrite lecteur,"* a phrase from Baudelaire, in a book he was giving to Will Barrett, but Barrett objected. When he finally gave me the book, I saw that he had written, For Anatole, from Delmore, in a microscopic hand.

I took the book home and read it over and over, trying to think of something good to say about it—but I needn't have worried, because he never asked me.

Delmore went into the dressing room and put on the suit. When he came out, the salesman buttoned the jacket and turned up the trouser cuffs. He tried to usher Delmore to the three-way mirror, but Delmore turned his back to it and asked me again, What do you think?

Delmore had a swaybacked stance that made the jacket gape at the collar and ride up on his belly, so that the skirts pulled together in front. Nobody ever looked less dressed in a suit. He could even turn buying a suit into a tragedy.

He had once been handsome, like poetry itself. I had seen early pictures of him, carefully lighted, shot on a slant, as if he was ascending, or descending. I believe there was sculpture behind him in one shot. But now he was heavy and you could see what he meant by "the withness of the body," or "the heavy bear who goes with me."

I gazed at him in the suit. What good could it do? I wondered. Can a suit make him sane? He ought to wear it just like that, with the trousers rolled and the jacket riding up in front.

He raised and lowered his arms. He shrugged his shoulders to settle the suit, but it wouldn't come right. How do I look? he asked.

Turn around, I said. Let me see the back. And behind his back, I made up my mind.

I thought that here on the sixth floor of Brooks Brothers, the salesman was the public, I was the critic and Delmore was the poet. I thought I saw dried shaving cream in one of Delmore's ears. I thought of a line by Tristan Tzara: "The lonely poet, great wheelbarrow of the swamps."

17

fter Sheri, I thought once again that now, at last, I
would have what people call a normal sex life. I felt
like a man who goes back to college after knocking
about the world in a tramp steamer. I saw myself as
someone who has been robbed of his youth—first by
the war and then by Sheri—and I wanted to be young
again. I wanted to be ordinary. I could hardly imagine
what sleeping with an ordinary girl would be like.

To someone who hasn't lived through it, it's almost
impossible to describe the sexual atmosphere of 1947.
To look back at it from today is like visiting a medieval
town in France or Italy and trying to visualize the life of
its inhabitants in the thirteenth century. You can see the
houses and the cathedral, the twisting streets, you can
read about the kind of work they did, the food they ate,
or about their religion, but you can't imagine how they
felt; you can't grasp the actual terms of their consciousness. The mood or atmosphere, the tangibility of their

lives, eludes you because we don't have the same frame of reference. It's as if the human brain and the five senses were at an earlier stage of development.

In 1947, American life had not yet been split open. It was still all of a piece, intact, bounded on every side, and, above all, regulated. Actions we now regard as commonplace were forbidden by law and by custom. While all kinds of things were censored, we hadn't even learned to think in terms of censorship, because we were so used to it. The social history of the world is, in some ways, a history of censorship.

Nineteen forty-seven was a time when any suggestion of extramarital sex in a movie had to be punished, just as crime had to be punished. To publish a picture of pubic hair was a criminal offense. *Lady Chatterley's Lover* and *Tropic of Cancer* were banned and *Portnoy's Complaint* was twenty-two years away. There was no birth-control pill, no legal abortion—yet none of this tells you what sex at that time was like. The closest I can come to it is to say that sex was as much a superstition, or a religious heresy, as it was a pleasure. It was a combination of Halloween and Christmas—guilty, tormented, clumsy, unexamined, and thrilling. It was as much psychological as physical—the *idea* of sex was often the major part of foreplay. A naked human body was such a rare and striking thing that the sight of it was more than enough to start our juices flowing. People were still visually hungry; there was no sense of déjà vu as there is now. As a nation, we hadn't lost our naïveté.

Of course, I'm talking about middle- and upper-middle-class people—that's where the girls I met came from. They were "good" girls whose sexuality had been shaped by their mothers and by the novels of George Eliot and Virginia Woolf, perhaps even Henry James. They wore padded bras and pantie girdles and they bought their bathing suits a size too large. The suggestion of a nipple through a sweater or a blouse or a panty seam through a skirt would have been considered pornographic.

Sex was the last thing such a girl gave a man, an ultimate or ultimatum. It was as much a philosophical decision on her part as an emotional one and it had to be justified on ethical and aesthetic grounds. To sleep with a man was the end of a long chain of behavior that began with calling yourself a liberal, with appreciating modern art—sex was a modern art—and going to see foreign films. Sex too was foreign. It was a postwar thing, a kind of despairing democracy, a halfhearted form of suicide. It was a freedom more than a pleasure, perhaps even a polemic, a revenge against history. Still, there had to be love somewhere in it too—if not love of a particular man, then love of mankind, love of life, love of love, of anything.

In a way I was just as inhibited as they were by my upbringing, which condemned me to a combination of boredom and desire. Like most young men, I hadn't yet learned how to just *be* with girls, to exist alongside them, to make friends—and so once my desire was satisfied, I was bored. To make it worse, I suffered from a kind of boyhood chivalry and politeness that kept me from being natural, so that I was acting all the time, and that was fatiguing. I was guiltily aware that I was using girls badly—yet to use them well would have been to love them, and I didn't have the time or space in my life for that. For all these reasons, there was always an aura of disappointment between us as we kept renewing a bad bargain.

In *Portnoy's Complaint,* Portnoy says that underneath their skirts girls all have cunts. What he didn't say—and this was his trouble, his real complaint—was that underneath their skirts they also had souls. When they were undressed, I saw their souls as well as their cunts. They wore their souls like negligés that they never took off. And one man in a million knows how to make love to a soul.

Sex in 1947 was like one of those complicated toys that comes disassembled, in one hundred pieces, and without instructions. It would be almost impossible for someone today to understand how far we were from explicit ideas like pleasure or gratification. We were more in the situation of Columbus wondering whether the world was flat or round. Because they didn't know how to make love, girls made gestures. They offered their idiosyncrasies as a kind of passion. In their nervousness, they brought out other, totally dissociated forms of extremity. They gave me their secret literature, their repressed poems and stories, their dances.

One of the things we've lost is the terrific *coaxing* that used to go on between men and women, the man pleading with a girl to sleep with him and the girl pleading with him to be patient. I remember the feeling of being incandescent with desire, blessed with it, of talking, talking wonderfully, like singing an opera. It was a time of exaltation, this coaxing, as if I was calling up out of myself a better and more deserving man. Perhaps this is as pure a feeling as men and women ever have.

What an effort we used to make. And how gladly, joyously, we made it. Nothing was too much, too preposterous. I remember one night, or rather a morning, a freezing January morning at about 2:00 A.M.—I was running through the dark, sleeping streets, running as fast as I could. I was wearing only a sweater, and I had no socks on. I didn't want to stop to put on socks. There was a girl in my apartment who insisted that I wear a condom and I was afraid she would change her mind and leave before I could get back from the all-night drugstore, which was half a mile away. I kept thinking of her as I ran, I saw her rising from the bed, pulling on her stockings, shaking her dress down over her head. I had wanted to take her dress or her shoes with me so she couldn't leave, but I thought this might antagonize her. Though she wasn't a girl whom I loved, I would have done anything for her that night. It was crazy, and I was aware that I was acting crazy as I ran through the streets—yet I kept running. Until we became sophisticated about it, sex was everything Freud said it was.

The energy of unspent desire, of looking forward to sex, was an immense current running through American life. It was so much more powerful then because it was delayed, cumulative, and surrounded by doubt. It was fueled by failures, as well as by successes. The force of it would have been enough to send a million rockets to the moon. The structure of desire was an immense cathedral arching inside of us. While sex was almost always disappointing in retrospect, the promise of it ennobled and abstracted us; it made us pensive.

Before sex was explained to us in the sixties, we had to explain it to ourselves, and our versions were infinitely better. Sex seemed so much more extreme before it was explained to us—we reached back into our imaginations and brought out the unheard-of. It was like the sex jokes I was told when we moved from New Orleans to Brooklyn. I was seven years old and when I went out into the street to play, the other kids told me sex jokes. Apart from the fact that I didn't know anything about sex, these jokes all had a surrealistic cast. They contained elements of fairy tales, science fiction, and horror movies.

Perhaps sex is most wonderful when it preserves a bit of that grotesqueness we all feel in the beginning. It's the surrealistic moments that frighten and elate you with a kind of impractical, unenactable love, a love that you can't bring down to earth. I remember a girl, for example, a modern dancer, who had studied with Martha Graham. One day in class Martha Graham had said, Girls, you must breathe with your vaginas. And this girl made up her mind to do this with me. She thought that if it was true for dancing, it must be true for sex too. What could be more natural? She told me that she had tried breathing with her vagina when she was alone and it was a marvelous feeling, like being lighter than air, like filling her lungs with sex. I was very turned on by the idea and I did my best to cooperate. But though we were energetic, it never happened. She was stubborn and she was strong, but at least she gave up. No, she said, her voice full of regret, I can't do it with you. She lay there thinking; her face was a diagram of thinking. Then she got out of bed and took up a position in front of the bookcase. I had painted the bookcase black and she looked magnificent against the black and the books. She drew herself up very straight—she was tall and muscular. I could see her gathering herself, her muscles rippling. I can't do it with you, she said, but I can do it by myself. Watch—give me a minute or two. She spread her feet a little and relaxed her knees. Now, she said, I'm doing it now. And she did—I saw her and there wasn't the slightest doubt in my mind.

With a girl, there was always the definition of terms: what getting into bed meant to her and what it could mean to me. Why are we doing this? she would ask, and I would have to make up a lie because I didn't know the answer. As we pressed up against the idea of love, as we felt its heat and blinked in its light, the personal and the philosophical met in a blur.

I would be seized with an incredible sincerity, and while I knew that this sincerity was temporary, there was a sense in which it was eternal too. The girl and I were like two bows bent all the way back, with only one arrow between us. Seduction was a touching and beautiful genre, the most heartfelt literature of the self. At such times, I saw myself as I might be, as lovable. And I think the girl saw herself at her best too, as inspiring.

There was a wonderful embarrassment about it all, a moral nakedness. A contemporary writer, a psychotherapist, defined embarrassment as radiance that doesn't know what to do with itself—and that's what we had. We had radiance. When people are embarrassed, it's as if they've fallen out of their compulsive rhythms and are framed for a moment in an absolute, undefended stillness.

Undressing was a drama in itself. A girl standing with her arms behind her back, at the clasp of her bra, had some of the beauty of a crucifixion. She also looked as if she was hiding something behind her, a gift. Pausing, gazing past me into the middle distance, her arms still back, handcuffed by hesitation and desire, she was trying to see the future or the end of love. And when at last her breasts sprang loose, she looked down at them with as much amazement as I did.

When a girl took off her underpants in 1947, she was more naked than any woman before her had ever been. It was as if time or history itself had been evolving toward her nakedness, yearning for it. The men of my generation had thought obsessively about her body, had been elaborately prepared for it, led up to it by the great curve of civilization. Her body was on the tip of our minds, a pinup on the brink of our progress, our freedom. We'd carried it, like a gun, all through the war. The nakedness of women was such an anticipated object that it was out in front of American culture, like the radiator ornament on the hood of a car. We were at that point in our social evolution where we had taken in as much awareness of women's bodies as we could stand without going mad. We were a nation of voyeurs.

Perhaps, when she had undressed, a girl would apologize for her body, say that it was too thin or fat, that her breasts were too small. It was always she who had to measure up, who had to justify men's furious imaginings. If she had dared to refer to it, she might have apologized for her sex—its wetness, its pungency, its hairiness, its peculiar, almost furtive location. She might end her undressing with a little shrug, as if to say, This is all I have.

I loved the awkwardness of these girls. There were times when it broke my heart. Afraid to take any sort of initiative, they hovered and fumbled, loitered and digressed. This awkwardness was, for me, a kind of sublime, an unconscious statement of their innocence. I remember a girl whose awkwardness took the form of stepping in dog shit in the street when we were on the way to my apartment. It happened three or four times and I asked her, Don't you see where you're going? But that was precisely what she didn't want to do. She didn't want to see. Stepping in dog shit was like retreating all the way back to the pregenital. It was a proof of her inadvertence, her sublimity.

One girl in particular sums up that time for me. She was a perfect example of what I mean when I say that sex used to be more individual, more personally marked, than it is now. She stands out beyond the others not because she was more original than they were, but because a combination of circumstances allowed her to spin out her idiosyncracy, to find what it needed.

Her name was Virginia and she was a rich girl who had come to New York to study art—not to paint or sculpt, but study, to *be with* art, to live near it. When she arrived in the Village, she made a great hit because she had high cheekbones. In 1947, high cheekbones were the best thing a girl could have, better than big breasts or great legs. Cubism had reached the human face and people in the Village liked to talk about bone structure.

What impressed me almost as much as her cheekbones was a remark Virginia made the first time we talked. She had told me that she was from a coastal town in New England and, trying to imagine the circumstances of her life, I asked her how close her house was to the water.

Quite close, she said. Close enough so that when I

lay in bed at night with the windows open I can distinguish the sound of the water lapping against the hull of my boat from that of the other boats. I thought this quite a fine distinction, like a piece of aquatic literary criticism. She had a low voice and a clipped, toothy way of talking.

On the strength of her cheekbones and that remark, I took her out. But her conversation was so polite, so relentlessly general, that I couldn't get up the necessary momentum, couldn't set in motion the kind of rhetoric that would have made it possible to ask her to come home with me. It was not until the fourth time we went out that I asked her. I gave up any idea of leading up to it and just asked. I hadn't even touched her, but I said, I want you to stay with me tonight.

Without appearing to hear what I said she told me that she had to exercise her dog. She had a saluki, a very fast and elegant breed that had to be run every day. I thought this meant taking the dog to Washington Square and throwing a stick, but Virginia had more style than that. We got into her MG, one of the early, rakish models, and the dog leapt gracefully onto the folded canvas top.

We drove to West Street, along the Hudson under the West Side Drive. In those days West Street was deserted at night. When Virginia stopped the car, the dog jumped out and sat on the cobblestones, waiting for a signal. Then, as we headed south, he loped easily alongside. The car was so low that his head was on a level with mine. He grinned as he ran and I noticed that he had high cheekbones, too.

I remember that there was a hugh garbage compactor on the dock at the foot of Twelfth Street and its smell mingled with the milder reek of the river, which we could glimpse between the rotting wharves. The MG was stiffly sprung and made a lot of noise drumming over the cobblestones. Virginia held her hands at three and nine o'clock on the polished wooden steering wheel.

West Street at night was the kind of place that makes you pensive. The ruined docks seemed to say that there would be no more steamer trunks and champagne in first-class cabins, or friends coming down to the dock to see you off to Europe. To take Virginia home with me would be like sailing from one of these docks. I looked at her and tried to estimate my chances, but she was wrapped up in her dog and her driving.

The docks reminded me of the one in Yokohama where I had scraped the shit away and there was a military suggestion about Virginia too. She wore a tweed suit whose jacket was cut in what was called an Eisenhower style, with a biswing back. In everything she did, she impressed me as obeying a mysterious discipline.

We drove south for about a mile, then turned north again. We did this twice and it was all perfectly solemn. We hardly spoke because of the wind in our ears and because the scene itself imposed a kind of silence. The third time around I noticed that the dog was tiring. His tongue was lolling and his stride had lost some of its grace.

I wondered how much farther Virginia meant to go. The vibration of the car was getting to my bladder and the dog was so done in that it seemed cruel to keep on. I was going to ask her to stop, but then I realized—I don't know how, but I knew—that she had forgotten about the dog. She was deciding whether to go home with me or not. Perhaps the car would run out of gas.

In the end, it was the dog who decided. When I

tapped Virginia on the arm and pointed to him, she stopped suddenly, the first break in the perfection of her driving. I thought I would have to lift the dog into the car, but with a last gallant effort he jumped to the canvas. Tired with running after this girl, almost panting myself, I knew how he felt.

Now, one way or the other, she would have to answer. I rested my case, because I didn't think it would do any good to try to persuade her. She would follow her own peculiar imperatives.

The car idled very fast, as if it was nervous. Virginia set the hand brake and then she pulled off her driving gloves. At least, I thought, her hands are naked, it's a beginning. Then she turned in the seat and stretched out one hand to the dog. She began to pet him, rubbing his ears, his head, his back. She went on rubbing, rubbing him for some time while I sat there gazing at the river shining between the wharves.

She was asking the dog what to do—what should she do? She was asking him to decide. And he said Yes, you need to run too. The night is made for running. She went home with me because the dog was so graceful, so brave. Perhaps we too would be graceful and brave. In her way Virginia was, though in the two or three months that I saw her she never said anything remotely resembling that remark about the water lapping against her boat.

The saddest part of sex in those days was the silence. Men and women hadn't yet learned to talk to one another in a natural way. Girls were trained to listen. They were waiting for history to give them permission to speak. They led waiting lives—waiting for men to ask them out, for them to have an orgasm, to marry or leave them. Their silence was another form of virginity.

There were all kinds of silences: timid silences, dogged silences, discreet, sullen, watchful, despairing silences, hopeful silences, interrogative silences. In the beginning, in the early stages of knowing a girl, I didn't mind, because desire was a kind of noise—but afterward, lying in bed, the silence was cold, as if we had no blanket to cover us. There were girls who insisted on kissing all through the act, and I thought of this kissing as a speechless babble.

I was so depressed by this silence, by the absence of real talk or genuine confiding, that I went around for a while with a deaf and dumb girl. Why not? I said to myself. Why not go all the way? I didn't know, when I picked her up in the lobby of the New School, that she couldn't hear. I assumed that her odd speech—the way of someone who has never heard speech—was the accent of a foreign student. It sounded like Arabic.

When I realized that she had been born this way it seemed like a judgment. I felt that I had reached a logical conclusion. This was the final silence between women and men—why go on pretending? Her hearing aid was in her bra—when she undressed, she was stone deaf. We could only tap each other on the arm. She told me that she heard my voice as a vibration in my chest.

There was another kind of silence: the silence of the body, not only in sex but in its other functions. I've known girls who never, even if they stayed a week at my apartment, had a bowel movement. If orgasm was difficult, excretion was impossible. And so these poor girls would be twice constipated, would have a double bellyache. In my small apartment, the toilet was too near, like the nearness of shame.

I could see the evidence of this withholding in their clouded eyes, their fading complexions, even their speech patterns. Their faces would get puffy, their bellies would be distended, their bodies knotted. Their sentences would clot as they longed to get away, to let go of it all.

If I had known how to reassure these girls, or if I had remained with any of them long enough, they might have relaxed and become natural with me, and I with them. But I was driven with restlessness. I was still looking for transfiguration, as I had said to Dr. Schachtel—it was transfiguration or nothing. But transfiguration had to start somewhere, and I never gave it a chance. There was another obstacle, too: I was just learning how to write, I turned everything into literature, and this was something no affair could survive.

Although their bodies were often beautiful to me and their personalities as appealing as our inhibitions allowed them to be, it was ultimately with girls' souls that I grappled. No matter what we said or did, I couldn't get away from their souls. Their souls lay beside us in the bed, watching, sorrowing. Perhaps I needed their souls—there is no other explanation for their inconvenient presence—but I didn't know what to do with them, any more than I knew what to do with my own.

I was looking for so much in each girl and she was looking for so much in me, we confused and depressed each other. I think too that I may have muddled sex and literature. The tension and the excitement were so similar that sometimes the two things were as difficult to distinguish as the tolling of distant church bells.